The World of LEGO® Toys

Henry Wiencek

Harry N. Abrams, Inc., Publishers, New York

Editor: Darlene Geis

Designer: Michael Hentges

Page 1: LEGO bricks, 1987
Pages 2 and 3: LEGO bricks, c. 1948

Photograph on page 9 by Hjalte Tin,
Denmark; photograph on page 108 by
Henner Prefi.

LEGO®, DUPLO®, LEGOLAND®,
FABULAND®, MODULEX®, and the
DUPLO and LEGO Logos® are registered
trademarks of, owned by, and used with
permission of the LEGO Group.

Copyright © 1987 Harry N. Abrams, Inc.

Times Mirror Books

Printed and bound in Japan

Library of Congress
Cataloging-in-Publication Data

Wiencek, Henry.
  The world of LEGO toys.

  Summary: A history of the successful toys,
LEGO bricks, describing some of the things
that can be built with them.
  1. LEGO toys—Juvenile literature.   [1. LEGO toys]
I. Title.
TS2301.T7W474   1987   688.7′2   86–32300
ISBN 0–8109–1790–4 (hc.)
ISBN 0–8109–2362–9 (pbk.)

Contents

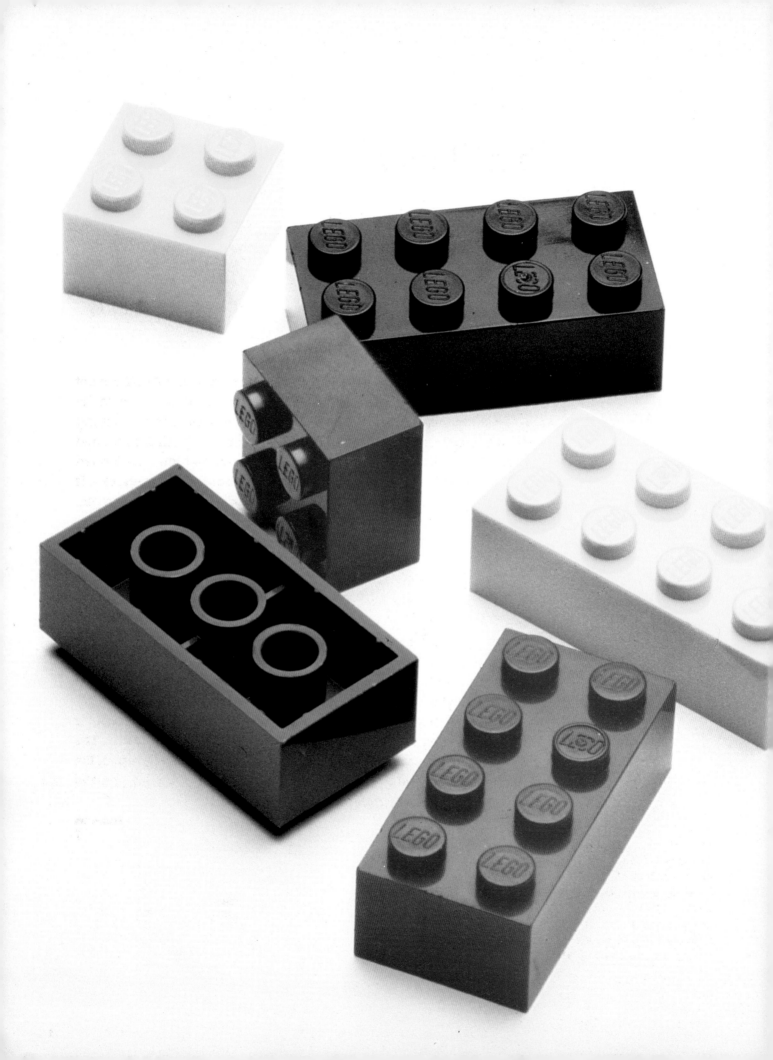

Introduction

If one of the powers of magic is the power to transform, then it is hard not to put LEGO bricks into the category of things touched by magic. In the hands of a child, a few bricks can become almost anything: a roaring lion, a prince's castle, a flying horse—or the family car. All the real and unreal shapes that the imagination can conjure are waiting to be formed in a box of these simple bricks. The possibilities are virtually endless. If you took half a dozen eight-stud LEGO bricks of the same color you could put them together in almost 103 million ways (102,981,500, to be precise). Just three bricks of the same color offer 1,060 combinations.

What is a LEGO brick? It is a rectangular piece of plastic, yellow, red, blue, black, grey, or white, hollow on the inside except for one or more tubes, with rows of studs on the top emblazoned with the tiny letters "LEGO." Take two bricks, push the top of one into the bottom of the other, and, presto, with a satisfying click they snap together. The studs are locked in firm embrace with the tubes. Tired of that arrangement? Then pull them apart—they separate easily—and put them together in a different way. You could do that for twenty years and the bricks would not wear out. But more important, children do it hour after hour, day after day, absorbed in the pleasure of creating an individual world of play. The LEGO brick is the raw material for a child's imagination to act upon, the building block of fantasy—a creative material on a par with clay, pen and pencil, papier-mâché, and wood.

The bedrock of the LEGO system of toys, and of the LEGO company, is the brick. At the press of a fingertip the studs of one brick mesh smoothly and firmly with the tubes of another and will hold tight until the bricks are pulled apart to make a new model. The ingenious stud-and-tube design gives the bricks remarkable stability—fifty-foot-high towers have been built from them—and their versatility is limited only by the imagination.

The LEGO brick crosses cultural and language barriers with ease. This tote bag was made in the 1960s for Japanese children. In the photo opposite, a New Guinean father in a remote settlement on the April River tries his hand at building with a set brought by Danish travelers. The man and his children ignored the pictures on the box and designed their own towers and animal figures on wheels.

LEGO bricks have been a phenomenal success. Every year the company produces over three billion bricks and other types of building elements at plants in Denmark, Switzerland, Brazil, South Korea, and the United States. A worldwide network of sales companies and sales agents sells LEGO products in one hundred and twenty-five countries. As many as three hundred million people have played with them, and every year the world's children spend four billion hours building with their bricks, according to the company's estimates. Because the brick is so simple, it is universally understood: the children of Asia, Africa, Europe, Australia, and the Americas all use the same bricks.

If the LEGO company had produced only its brick, its fame and success would probably be secure; but they have not rested on their bricks. They have created a mini-universe of toys for children from the age of three months to adolescence. The BASIC sets—the bedrock of the LEGO range—encourage free-form creativity. There are also house-building sets that have realistic elements such as windows, shutters, doors, flowers, trees, and sloping components to form roofs. There are fantasy sets with which children can build medieval castles and spaceships. With advanced LEGO construction sets children fashion motorized mechanical contrivances out of gears, pulleys, hinges, and hand-driven pumps that compress air and make parts move.

A diminutive LEGO fireman, wielding a water hose and ready for action, stands proudly by his truck. The ladder swivels and extends, and the "Light and Sound" elements on top of the truck flash and make the sound of a siren.

Recent innovations include "Light and Sound" bricks that flash, beep, and make the sound of a police siren. The battery connection for these bricks was ingeniously designed without exposed wires. The educational products line includes sensors that detect light or touch, designed to be connected to a computer. For children at the youngest level of the age scale there are oversize bricks that very little hands can hold, and rattles for infants. Altogether, the LEGO company produces more than 1,200 different elements, and from the simplest to the most advanced, virtually everything fits together—you could make a computerized LEGO robot that shakes the baby's rattle. The whole complex variety of LEGO toys is not a random gathering of elements, but a coherent and very carefully planned system—a vast system devoted to fun, creativity, and stimulating, educational play.

A simple house has universal appeal. The colorful LEGO brick bungalow under construction features windows and doors that swing open and a garden with dainty flowers and sturdy pine trees.

LEGO® WORLD SHOW

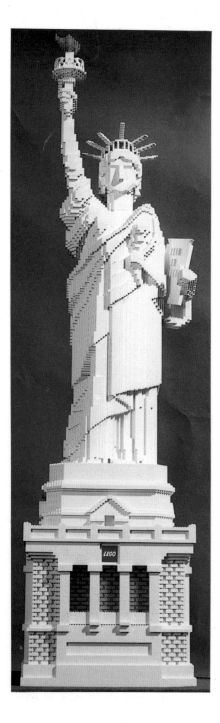

Models of famous buildings, landmarks, spaceships, and inventions travel around the world to demonstrate that there is no limit to what can be built with LEGO bricks. The models in the LEGO World Shows are painstakingly crafted in shops at Billund, Denmark, and Enfield, Connecticut. The Statue of Liberty is a perennial crowd-pleaser, and viewers are always surprised at the architectural accuracy of such models as Independence Hall.

Overleaf: The enormous model of the U.S. Capitol draws the biggest crowds and the loudest gasps of surprise. A triumph of craftsmanship in LEGO bricks, the replica was created by Dagny Holm, one of the chief designers in Denmark. It is so large that it must be shipped in sections and assembled at the display site.

Hilsen fra Billund

The source of all this material is the small town of Billund in Denmark, situated in the farming country at the center of the Jutland peninsula. The LEGO company was founded there in 1932 by the town carpenter, Ole Kirk Christiansen. After he turned from carpentry to toy making, his first products were hand-painted wooden cars, animals, and pull-toys. Although it now sells its products worldwide and employs some 6,000 people, the company remains where it was born, and still bears the conservative stamp of a small-town, farming culture. Ole Kirk's first clients were his neighbors, and any shoddy work would have meant swift failure. That sense of responsibility to the community may be one reason for the LEGO company's success. It is committed to making a product that is useful and of the highest quality. The company cares nothing for fads, knowing that there is no market more volatile than the toy market. For example, the company has produced no war toys: there are no LEGO tanks spitting shells, nor motorized robot warriors from the LEGO planet.

The LEGO company began in the small Danish village of Billund, where its vast factory and the headquarters building are now located. Although the town has grown, it retains its quiet, rural character, much as it was in this postcard from the 1920s.

A brightly striped duck was built by an eleven-year-old boy. He used hinges to make the duck's wings flap, but there is nothing in the LEGO system that can produce a recognizable "quack."

The company's guiding principle, almost from its earliest days, was Only the Best Is Good Enough. That motto was hand-carved on a wooden plaque in the 1940s by Ole Kirk's son Godtfred and hung on the wall of the workshop. This ethic of the handcraftsman was later applied to the mass production of plastic, a material that can lend itself to shoddy work unless care is taken. But the LEGO company takes toys, and children, seriously.

Children are not only consumers, a mass market to be wooed, but a very important group of people whose special needs are not always understood by adults. Adults often do not comprehend the importance of children's toys, and the role that toys play in a child's life. A toy is not just a colorful object that keeps a child occupied and quiet. Toys and play are the means by which children learn about themselves and the world, and develop their senses. Children are intensely interested in the way the world works—everything they see is new and wondrous to them. It is no accident that most toys are miniature versions of real objects—houses, kitchens, cars, farms—it is through playing with toys that children become familiar with the world, on a small scale.

Because the system is so adaptable, LEGO bricks are the ideal material for talented children, but also for children who cannot draw, paint, sculpt, mold clay, or figure out how to make something recognizable out of papier-mâché. With unskilled hands, a child can still make a perfectly respectable creation merely by pushing bricks together. The bricks enable even the most inartistic child to be an artist. The technical sets make any child into an engineer, junior grade. Want to build a model car that really runs? No problem—here are the bricks, gears, and motor, and a colored diagram to follow. Just put them together according to the plan, or follow your own creative instincts.

These two models—an elephant with a swinging trunk and a tightrope walker on wheels—were made of basic LEGO bricks by children who followed their own fancy rather than the instructions on the box.

Working with LEGO bricks is not "building by the numbers." A child can make the house or car pictured on the box, but he or she can also make a cup, an animal, or one of the indescribable objects that pop so easily out of a child's imagination. At a nursery school in New York, one three-year-old girl stacked five LEGO bricks and put a window on top from a LEGO house set. When asked if it was a house, she said, "No, it's a theater. This is the screen [she pointed to the window] and when I put my finger on one of these buttons [the studs on a brick] the people come on the screen. And when I put my finger on this button the puppets come out." So out of half a dozen pieces she had fashioned a fantasy theater that was sometimes a movie theater and sometimes a puppet show. She spent half an hour pressing the "buttons" and acting out stories that she made up.

In 1984 the company printed photographs of several models built by children, aged four to twelve, who had followed their own inspiration. There was a red elephant, with a wheel ingeniously standing in for the creature's curling tail. The eleven-year-old builder found an equally clever solution for the problem of creating a flexible trunk out of inflexible bricks: he attached a LEGO hinge at the top so the trunk could

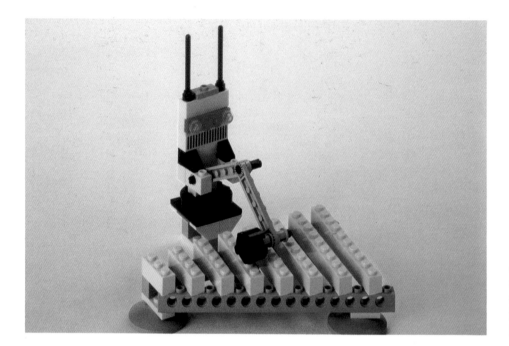

A child's imagination can create the most unlikely creatures. One clever young builder invented a robot that lulls children to sleep.

swing back and forth (though it cannot collect peanuts). Another eleven-year-old used hinges to allow his duck's wings to flap. An eight-year-old girl came up with a fanciful vehicle that must have been inspired by a visit to the circus—it was a long, narrow truck (driven by a pig!) with a pair of tall masts supporting a tightrope. But in place of the tightrope walker she put a tightrope rider, a LEGO figure, holding a cotton swab as a balancing pole, standing on a brick with a wheel that rolled along the tightrope.

Almost daily, the company receives a letter from some distant corner of the world announcing that a new object has been created from LEGO bricks by a youthful tinkerer. A fifteen-year-old American boy from the Midwest wrote that he was working on a model of the *Queen Mary* when news of the discovery of the *Titanic* wreck caused him to change his plans. He built an enormous model of the ill-fated liner in yellow, red, and blue, with an interior containing first-class cabins, lounges, a chapel, dining room, and engine room.

A number of the amateur designs have been mechanical devices of surprising sophistication. A thirteen-year-old Danish boy who was learning to knit in school grew tired of having to pull the yarn from the ball, so he designed a mechanical wool-puller. Another thirteen-year-old

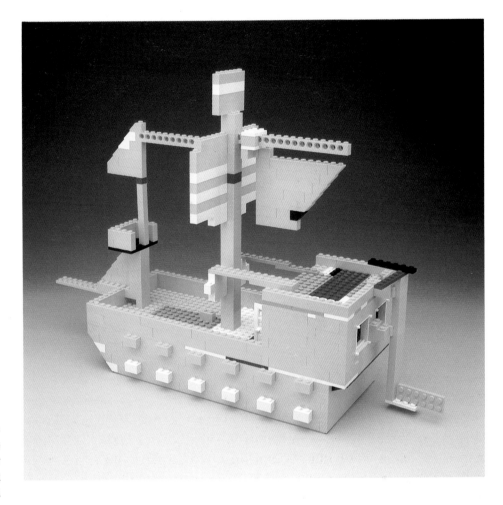

An eight-year-old boy's imagination took him to the high seas. He built a sturdy galleon with a rudder, deck space ample enough for a whole crew of swashbucklers, and a plank at the ship's bow, from which the pirates' enemies could be dispatched to their watery graves.

boy invented a different labor-saving device for himself, a motorized lawn-watering machine. He designed a sturdy platform to hold the hose, and a wheel-and-gear arrangement that would haul the hose slowly across the lawn—presumably freeing him to spend more time with his LEGO bricks.

A fourteen-year-old boy wrote a letter to the company describing how he had built a radio-controlled LEGO car. Like a true inventor, he was inspired by pure curiosity: "Would it be possible to build a radio-controlled LEGO car?" he wrote. "This question fascinated me." He designed his own chassis, transmission, and steering system; and after one spectacular smashup caused by a defect in his steering design, he succeeded in making a car that could turn and back up, with a top speed of fifteen miles an hour.

Outer space is crowded with a variety of bizarre LEGO vehicles inspired by fact and fantasy. This ship is part machine and part dragon. The crew has its quarters in the belly of the dragon.

For pure whimsy, nothing could beat the LEGO brick robot that eats spaghetti. The two-foot-tall creature, built by a thirteen-year-old Danish boy, "chews" spaghetti, "digests" it, and ejects the digested bits of pasta onto a trolley that rolls out on rails from his back. The robot also walks, turns, carries things in its hands, and flashes its green eyes in pleasure after a meal.

The company periodically sponsors model-building competitions, which are inundated with entries. In 1982 the LEGO company in Germany ran a contest in which children were invited to send in designs for models that had fifteen or fewer pieces. The purpose of the contest was to refute the idea that the system had grown too complex for children to enjoy. To their amazement, they got 5,000 entries, including a ten-year-old boy's design for a LEGO car powered by air rushing from a balloon attached at the rear. At a LEGO exhibition in 1982, the British company (which runs a LEGO fan club with 40,000 members) sponsored a competition for cars powered by a single rubber band. The winning entry beat several hundred other competitors by traveling a distance of sixty yards on one twist of the band.

Although not as sophisticated as the robot that eats spaghetti, this mobile Tomati-Spaghetto, built by a nine-year-old boy, reveals a definite creative flair. It can serve spaghetti, which it grips with its claw, while it pours tomato sauce out of a hose and sprinkles parmesan cheese with a shovel.

Two notable records were set by Britain's LEGO brick fanatics who constructed the world's largest greeting card out of bricks and the world's tallest toy structure. The tower, 15.3 meters high (just over fifty feet), was built in the course of several days at a LEGO toy fair in August, 1983. A tower made in London in 1985 was slightly shorter but set the world's record for a structure built within twenty-four hours.

At the same exhibition, the LEGO company in Britain enlisted its fans to create the world's largest greeting card to commemorate the birth of Prince William to Princess Diana and Prince Charles. For a donation of fifty pence (destined for the Princess' charitable trust), a child got a LEGO base plate on which he could design whatever he liked. In all, 320 children took part in the project, and their greetings were fitted together to create a giant card measuring about nine feet high and seven feet wide. The individual LEGO brick greetings tended toward the "Good Luck Will" and "Hello Bill" variety, with lots of smiling faces, a crown, and a few Union Jacks. Some of the children spelled out their own names on their plaques in a bid for royal recognition, and one child used bricks to spell out the cryptic message "Finger Power." Naturally, the card made the 1983 edition of *The Guinness Book of World Records*. It was never actually mailed, but the royal couple did see it at an exhibition.

The LEGO brick's British enthusiasts are adept at setting world records in the toy category. In 1985 they set the Guinness record for "the world's tallest toy construction built in twenty-four hours" with a 15.1-meters (about fifty feet) high, tower built in London's Waterloo Station. Tower-building is a passion of LEGO fans everywhere; it seems that every country must construct one, with or without a time limitation, and must record how high it went. In 1984 two Swedish teenagers pooled their bricks and built a tower so slender that it looked as if it would topple at any moment. But it stayed up long enough for the boys to take its measure—5.56 meters (over eighteen feet), a Swedish record at the time.

Andrew and Stephen Hyland, the 1985 "Bird Brains of Britain," won the annual BBC competition for the best bird-feeding devices, which they constructed from LEGO bricks. The boys are shown here with their feeders and the coveted "Bird Brain" trophy.

For unbridled LEGO enthusiasm, no one can best the British, who have gone so far as to develop a secret code based on the shapes and colors of the bricks, and who have a building contest in the pages of their LEGO Club magazine, *Bricks 'n' Pieces*, four times a year. In a 1985 issue, two brothers were featured for attaining an unusual honor through their cleverness with LEGO bricks: they had been chosen by the BBC as the "Bird Brains of Britain." Every year the television program "Wild Track" runs a contest for the most ingenious bird feeding device, but it cannot be any kind of bird feeder, it must *test* the bird. The devices are supposed to incorporate some trick or puzzle that a bird must figure out before it can get any food. The two boys were the only contestants to build feeders out of LEGO bricks. One of the feeders they devised included a colored wheel, on which the bird had to peck the correct color; another device forced the hungry bird to turn a wheel in order to get a single peanut. For their originality, the brothers won a trophy consisting of a blue tit perched on a milk bottle, and the right to call themselves the Bird Brains of Britain for one year.

A six-year-old girl created a graceful "Bird of Paradise," cleverly using a hinged element to make the strong but slender neck.

A Japanese boy is held aloft with his trophy after taking top honors in his age group at the first international building competition, held at Billund in 1984.

Japanese model builders of all ages have shown a flair for creating unusual items. At a 1980 exhibition in Tokyo, which attracted entries from schools and old-age homes, there was a chair with a pyramid-shaped seat, "for unwelcome guests," and a witty model of a man thinking. A thought balloon above his head was filled with a complex arrangement of gears and chains, powered by a gear in the man's head.

Adults also feel the allure of the LEGO brick. Because the bricks are toys, they give adults the all-too-rare chance to indulge their sense of play, which unleashes their creativity and allows some quite serious work to get done. Architects have used LEGO bricks to design fantasy houses. Sculptors and conceptual artists have created works that deliberately question the boundary between art and play. And hundreds of amateur builders around the world have found themselves swept up in an uncontrollable enthusiasm for building things.

A yellow spaceman surveys the surface of the moon from his observation platform aboard a rover designed by a seven-year-old boy.

A group of Finnish scientists from the University of Technology at Tampere built a computer-driven LEGO robot that eats coins and laughs at whoever is foolish enough to give it money. The robot is activated when a coin is dropped into a slot, which trips the program. A bucket catches the coin as it drops through the slot, and carries it to a conveyor, which in turn guides the coin to safekeeping in the cash box. When the coin has been deposited, the robot emits a cheerful, tape-recorded guffaw.

A North Dakota man designed a miniature, motorized LEGO brick combine (a harvesting machine) with a two-speed transmission, a straw-chopper, an auger that swings out, and a harvesting header that can be raised and lowered at the touch of a lever next to the driver's seat.

The company's staff of professional model makers—proudly called Master Builders—created this replica of a New England Victorian house with its steep gables and exuberant bands of color decorating the exterior. It has been a feature of the popular LEGO Americana Road Show.

Two imaginative and dogged American LEGO fanatics are Gary Istok and Michael Burton. In Burton's Grosse Pointe, Michigan home the two men (both in their thirties) are constructing a six-hundred-square-foot city of bricks. They plan to recreate the architectural ambience of an old European city, with a mixture of modern, nineteenth-century, and medieval styles. They have already built a yellow-and-black baroque city hall, with a tower and four-columned portico; a Gothic cathedral in red and black; an Art Deco office building with graceful arched entrances; a modern office complex that could compete with the designs of professional architects; a department store; a hospital; and a train station. One of their finest designs is an elegant opera house made of white bricks with friezes of blue and red, and more than one hundred windows.

Istok and Burton base their designs on real buildings, but they do not copy any of them exactly. They look at photographs of buildings (Burton has a collection of one thousand picture postcards), borrow an element here and an idea there, and create something fresh out of their imagination. Needless to say, they are enormous consumers of LEGO bricks: Burton has placed orders for as many as twenty-eight thousand elements at a time.

Constructing one of the technical LEGO models is a totally absorbing experience, akin to solving an elaborate puzzle or unraveling a mystery. It seems impossible that a box of bricks, beams, gears, motor, and elastic bands (for use as drive belts), can be transformed into a tractor, or a bulldozer. A set of LEGO model instructions is as finely plotted as a spy novel: the first steps, like the first pages of a thriller, seem completely irrelevant to the outcome. In its early stages, a model almost never looks anything like what it is going to be (but if you took a real car apart, how many of its sections would be recognizable?), and in that element of the unexpected lies part of the appeal, the lure of LEGO brick building. You put yourself in the hands of the designers, the authors of this construction "plot," and press on, suspending disbelief and feeling that you are being introduced to the secret structure of things. You cannot restrain yourself from continuing, because you have to see how this construction plot will come out.

Following the instructions, which are entirely pictorial (no words are ever used) and as accurate as blueprints, requires very close attention to detail. You can't just look at the drawing of the finished car and snap the bricks together by intuition. You quickly learn, for example, that when a short brick is to be snapped on top of a long beam that you have to put it in precisely the right place. You do this by counting studs. You look at the diagram, count the studs from the end of the beam to the edge of the brick, and snap the brick exactly onto those studs. The joy of working with these pieces is that you don't have to be particularly good with your hands—you don't have to saw a piece at just the right angle or apply just the right amount of glue at exactly the right spot—you merely snap pieces together.

As the object takes shape, step by step, your concentration deepens and excitement grows. You attach a gear, then another, and another. On goes the motor—then the maddening interlude (a digression in the plot) when you must laboriously piece together a long drive chain out of the tiniest links. You loop the chain over the motor and a gear, you turn on the motor, and lo! The gears all spin merrily away. But they are not yet connected to anything (and it's already past midnight). You cannot stop. You flip the pages of the instructions to peek at the end. Only five more steps. How can it be? The piece is still so formless.

If you are building one of the "pneumatic" models, with a two-inch air pump and little lengths of plastic hose, your task is doubly absorbing. The hoses must be threaded just so, through precisely *those* holes in the beams, around *this* brick and *that* axle, until they find their destination at the switching box. You try a few test pumps, and sink in despair; it won't work. But you have come this far and you know you have faith in the designer now; it *must* work. You run your eyes through the maze of beams and find the spot where the hose has kinked. You straighten it out, pump again, and success! It works!

When you snap the final pieces into place you eagerly turn on the motor, and your creation jerks to mechanical life: the crane lifts, or the car zips along the floor, or your bulldozer solemnly raises and lowers its shovel. Like Dr. Frankenstein, you have assembled the random parts of nature and magically animated them. You taste the euphoria of the inventor. You may not have designed it, but you doggedly traveled in the footsteps of the inventor, and you comprehend the essence of this machine. You are an expert now, and if someone asked you how this thing works you could knowledgeably point out its mechanisms. And you also begin to see how else you could apply your newfound mechanical knowledge. This car, suitably modified, could carry the sugar bowl across the table, or deliver a glass of beer from kitchen to den. It is of no importance that the end result is merely a little toy tractor—you are a *builder*, and you avidly flip through the instructions for an even more complex task, anticipating the pleasure of play you thought only children could enjoy.

___

32

This space-traveling robot carries two astronauts on imaginary journeys to the stars, with flashing lights and unearthly sound effects provided by the "Light and Sound" elements in his belly.

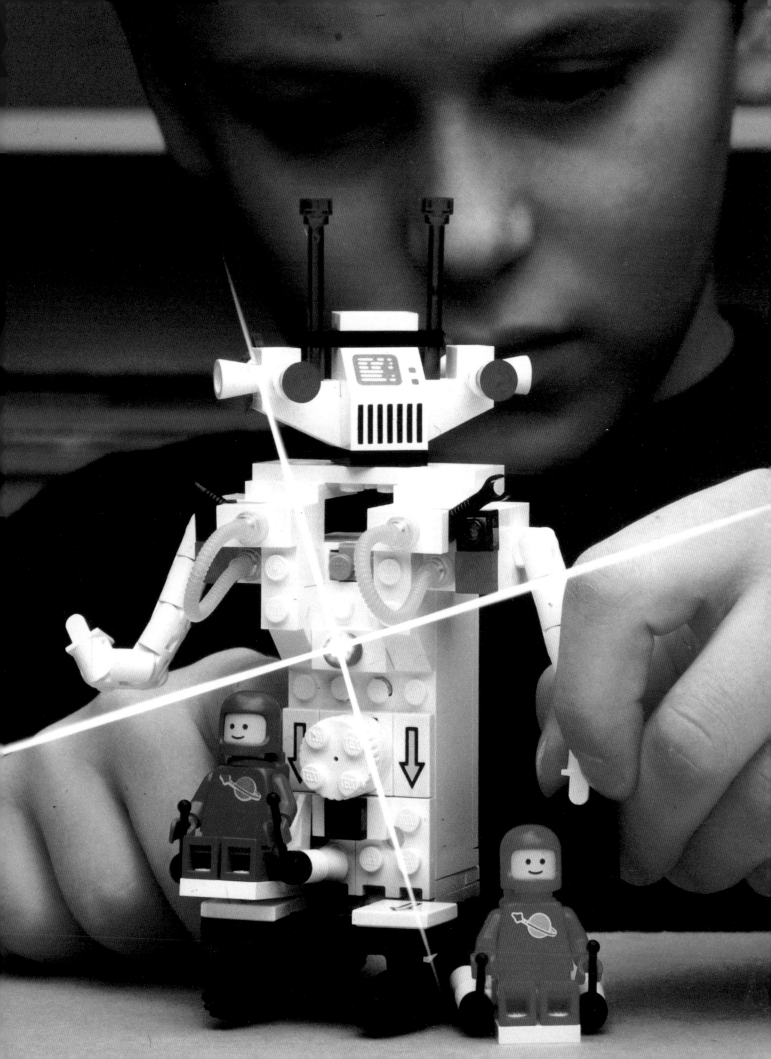

The Birth of the Brick

The LEGO system has been developed in the course of three decades by a legion of designers, but the company has always been under the direction of a single family, the Kirk Christiansens, who founded it. Because the company continues to be family-owned and -run, it has not wavered from its original principles—to create the best possible system of play for children, regardless of what the market demands.

The character of the company was formed in its early decades, the 1920s to the 1940s, when it rose from the humblest origins. The founder, Ole Kirk Christiansen, was born in 1891 in the village of Filskov, just to the northwest of Billund. The landscape around Billund looks much the same today as it has for centuries. Moors surround the town, and the view, when it is not obscured by the region's notorious autumnal fog, is of flat, green land. It is farming, grazing, and dairy land, worked by industrious people who have long been used to managing with little in the way of comforts and luxuries.

Ole Kirk's family was poor, and in the custom of the times he was put to work as soon as he was able to take care of himself. At the age of six he was given the job of keeping watch over flocks of sheep on the moors, a cold and lonely task that the boy made a bit more tolerable by practicing his whittling.

When his talent for working with wood was noted by his parents, he was apprenticed to an older brother who was a carpenter and joiner. After learning the basics of the carpenter's trade, he traveled to Germany and Norway to work. In 1916, when he was twenty-five, he returned to Billund and bought a woodworking and carpentry shop with the wages he had saved. The town had only recently been reached by the railroad line, and the year after Ole Kirk's return it got its first electric

Ole Kirk Christiansen founded the LEGO company in Billund. His original carpentry shop was located in the white building with the single chimney on the right. Later, in the 1930s when his business grew and workmen had to haul loads of toys through the streets at night, Ole Kirk installed rubber wheels on the delivery carts so as not to disturb his neighbors.

power station. Despite these improvements, Billund was a backwater, a "forsaken railway stopping point where nothing could possibly thrive," as one person described it in the 1920s, when the population was only a few hundred or so. Picture postcards of the time show rows of neat, simple houses lining the dirt road that ran through town. The tallest structure was the brick chimney on the town dairy, which Ole Kirk built.

His main business was working on houses and making furniture for the region's farmers. Even in good times the farmers were often strapped for cash and unable to pay their bills. Ole Kirk was always close to the edge with his own creditors, and more than once he had to send an apprentice rushing off to the bank at the last minute to make the payment that would keep him out of bankruptcy. But he did not let money interfere with his sense of community purpose. When he contracted to build a church during World War I, soaring prices for increasingly scarce materials caused him to lose money on the project. He went ahead and built the church at the agreed price, saying only, "It's all in a good cause."

A 1920s photograph of Ole Kirk, posing proudly with his wife and three of their four sons, shows a handsome, sturdy man in a neat moustache, wearing a fine dark suit. Two of those sons, Godtfred and Karl Georg, dealt Ole Kirk a temporary setback in 1924. One Sunday afternoon the boys lit the fire in a glue melter in the workshop. A pile of wood shavings ignited, and flames quickly spread through the shop and the Kirk Christiansens' house. The family was able to escape in time, but the home and shop were ruined.

The trait that enabled Ole Kirk to withstand these setbacks and the adversities to come was an almost unshakable self-confidence, a confidence that was grounded upon his strong religious faith. In an interview in 1986, Godtfred Kirk Christiansen said: "My father's faith in God, which was evident in everything he did, helped carry him through the difficulties that beset the family and the firm in the early years. His faith made him an active man, it gave him courage and solace. He was determined and persevering—and optimistic, too. Looking back today, I think his approach to life can best be expressed in his own words to his children: 'Life is a gift, but it's more than just that—life is a challenge.'"

37

These photographs, from the Kirk Christiansen family album, show (from top) Ole Kirk in 1911 with the bicycle he bought after completing his apprenticeship as a carpenter and joiner; Ole Kirk, his wife, Kirstine, and three of their sons in 1924 (Godtfred is at the left); Billund in the 1920s; Ole Kirk and his sister, about 1910; the combined home and shop Ole Kirk built after the first one burned down; and pages from Ole Kirk's "character book," in which employers wrote comments on his performance and personal habits when he was an apprentice.

Immediately after the fire had destroyed his home and workshop, Ole Kirk turned the disaster into an opportunity to expand. He hired an architect to design a much larger building than he had occupied before, an impressive, two-story brick structure. This grand space was not meant for himself: he lodged his family in a small, cramped flat, took a few rooms for his office and shop, and rented out the rest of the building.

When the Depression hit Denmark in the early 1930s the farmers were among those most severely affected. Ole Kirk's carpentry business dwindled, forcing him to lay off his workers. When he gave one employee his paycheck in 1931, Ole Kirk told him to "cash it at the co-op store, but tell [the manager] not to send it to the bank for three months!"

With no new houses going up, he concentrated his production on ironing boards and stepladders. In order to eliminate waste in the production process, he first made small, scale models of his products, to find out exactly what parts he would have to manufacture and to ensure that they would fit and work properly. This practical instinct for thoroughness led to an inspiration—if he could make miniature ironing boards and ladders, why not make toys?

He began making wooden buses, animal pull-toys, piggy banks, tiny baby carriages for dolls, and other toys. A 1932 group photo of the seven-person work force shows them posing with Ole Kirk's incongruous line of products—an airplane perches atop a ladder, and a bus is parked on top of an ironing board. The toys themselves seemed to exude the confidence Ole Kirk had in himself, even in the difficult times of the Depression: he built sleek little roadsters and coupés, painted in vivid colors. He made a fire truck with a ladder that could be raised and extended, and a little cart drawn by a yellow duckling that waddled along on webbed feet as the child pulled it across the floor. His miniature airplanes and trains proclaimed a faith in progress and the certainty that better times would come.

39

Before the LEGO company perfected the plastic building brick, the firm had earned a reputation for making superb wooden toys, which were manufactured until 1960. Godtfred Kirk Christiansen, son of the founder, designed these two cars and the post-office truck in the late 1930s.

Overleaf: Among the amusing pull toys manufactured by the LEGO company in the 1940s were a dog-and-wagon combination and a cart with a chubby clown hunched over handlebars. The clown bobs up and down as the cart is pulled along. Note the early LEGO logo on these toys.

A wholesaler, impressed with Ole Kirk's designs, placed a large order, believing that the farmers would want to buy these inexpensive toys to keep their children from feeling the pinch of poverty so keenly. The wholesaler went bankrupt, and Ole Kirk was stuck with the whole consignment. He loaded trucks and ducks, planes and trains into his old Ford and drove around the region, exchanging his toys for whatever the farmers could give him. Since cash was scarce he accepted food, even, in one case, taking a sack of almonds.

Facing bankruptcy himself in 1932, he asked his nine sisters and brothers to lend him money, which they did, along with the stern advice that he start making something more useful than toys. Nevertheless, Ole Kirk continued with his toy line, but he also manufactured practical milking stools, Christmas tree bases, and his full-size ladders and ironing boards. He made a chancy investment in a planing machine from Germany that cost more than his entire year's earnings.

In the mid-1930s Ole Kirk had his first brush with a toy fad—the yo-yo. Like the rest of the world, Denmark was suddenly gripped by a craze for these toys, and Ole Kirk had his men working around the clock to turn them out. He shipped them by the night train, and had the hand-carts in which they were trundled to the station equipped with rubber wheels so they wouldn't disturb the villagers' sleep. But just as suddenly as the yo-yo craze arrived, it collapsed, and Ole Kirk found himself with a shop full of yo-yos and no one to buy them. Again, inspiration struck. He split the yo-yos in half and used the halves as wheels for a new toy truck, which made an immediate hit with Danish children.

From the start, Ole Kirk had been firmly committed to top quality in design and construction. It was at this time that the company motto, Only the Best Is Good Enough, was born. Some time later, his son Godtfred had the opportunity to see the words put into action. One day in the late 1930s he conceived the smart idea of saving money by omitting the second coat of paint on a shipment of toys. Quite pleased with himself, he told Ole Kirk how much money he had saved, and was surprised when his father demanded that he recall the shipment and repaint every toy.

42

Ole Kirk's joiners and painters produced toys of the highest quality and durability. This sleek roadster, delicate pram, and waddling duck endured years of rough play from little hands, but the toys remain in remarkably good condition after five decades. The duck was the company's best-selling toy from the mid-1930s to the late 1940s.

These soundly built wooden sailboats exemplify the high level of craftsmanship the toys attained in the 1940s. When the company began producing plastic toys, it maintained its commitment to quality.

In 1934 Ole Kirk held a little contest to find a name for his company, offering a bottle of his own homemade wine as the prize. He had been considering two names: LEGIO, based on the Latin word legion, which would be appropriate because he intended to create a legion of toys, and LEGO, a word he coined from the Danish phrase *leg godt* (play well). None of the other entries could beat the word that suggested good playing, so Ole Kirk got to drink the prize himself. It was only after he had selected the name that he discovered that LEGO in Latin means "I put together," or "I assemble."

The partially painted baby rattle, shown with the designer's sketch for the final product, was one of the company's first plastic items. The designer was Ole Kirk's son Godtfred, known in the company as GKC.

After World War II, plastic began to come into wide use. Though the LEGO company had made its reputation in Denmark with high-quality wooden toys, Ole Kirk recognized the future when he saw it. In 1947 he bought a machine and molds for producing plastic toys. Among the first items he produced was a plastic baby's rattle. In 1949 the company offered a plastic tractor that a child could take apart and put together again, launching the concept of "additional play value," which would later be one of the underpinnings of the LEGO system. Though plastic had a reputation for flimsiness, Ole Kirk sought to bring out the best in that material. He believed that a toy is of no use "if it breaks an hour after the child gets it."

1949 was the revolutionary year for the company—it was in that year that the company introduced something then called the "automatic binding brick." For years Ole Kirk had been making wooden blocks in the traditional European style—simple, handmade cubes that could be stacked one on top of the other. When he began producing plastic toys he copied the old wooden design in the new material, but the plastic cubes didn't seem quite right. Plastic offered special creative possibilities for toy design, and the Kirk Christiansens, with their restless urge to improve their products, wanted to take advantage of those possibilities: the question was, how to do it. As Godtfred recalled: "It occurred to us that the bricks would become an even better toy, with an even wider range of possibilities, if they could be 'locked' together. What emerged from that idea was several rather primitive prototypes, in a variety of sizes, of what was later to become the real LEGO brick."

The "automatic binding brick," despite its somewhat cumbersome name, was a remarkably simple, yet extraordinarily versatile toy. It was a plastic brick with studs on the top that fit into the hollow of a brick placed above it. The bricks fit together snugly enough to stay connected, but not so tightly that they could not be taken apart. It was the birth of the LEGO brick.

As with many new products, the plastic brick was not well received at first. Many shipments were returned from the stores unsold, and a Danish trade magazine was disgruntled enough to write, "Plastics will never take the place of good, solid wooden toys!"

46

The first, rather primitive LEGO brick, made in 1949, was called the "automatic binding brick." It had studs on the top and was notched at the sides to provide flexibility, but it had no tubes underneath. The tubes were added in 1958.

Undaunted by the poor reception, the Kirk Christiansens stuck by their brick. Its fortunes underwent a sea change in 1954, as the result of a chance encounter on the North Sea ferry between Godtfred Kirk Christiansen (by then junior managing director of the LEGO company, and known throughout the company by his initials, GKC) and a buyer from a Copenhagen department store. Both men were en route to England to attend a toy fair. After a general discussion of toys, the buyer lamented that there was no toy *system* on the market, no toy with a really good concept behind it. The buyer's remarks intrigued GKC, who took them as a sort of challenge. After several months of thought, he drew up a list of ten basic qualities that a good LEGO product should possess:

Unlimited play potential
For girls and boys
Fun for every age
Year-round play
Healthful, quiet play
Long hours of play
Development, imagination, creativity
The more toys, the greater their value
Extra sets available
Quality in every detail

As GKC recalled: "With these basic rules in mind—and they still apply to this day throughout the LEGO Group—we made a thorough analysis of all existing LEGO products in wood and plastic [some two hundred in all]. What we were looking for was a product made up of a few components but with a healthy potential—an international product, that lent itself to mass production. It eventually began to look as though the product with the greatest promise was our early type of LEGO brick. If we could improve it from the technical point of view *and* develop a system for it, we could well have our future LEGO product."

Early LEGO sets, produced in the 1950s, were among the first to feature the automatic binding brick. The colorful boxes are fairly bursting with the promise of fun—the children on the covers are too busy enjoying themselves to look up—and the buildings shown on the boxes demonstrate the marvels that can be made with the new bricks. The boy in the white shirt is Kjeld Kirk Kristiansen, grandson of the company founder and today the president of the LEGO Group.

GKC and his associates then got down to the task of conceiving a system of play based on the brick. What emerged from their brainstorming was a system that would give children the opportunity to create complicated and interesting constructions. Using the new LEGO system, boys and girls could build entire towns out of LEGO bricks, and complete their fantasies with vehicles of all kinds, signs, and even trees. One of the more ambitious early sets allowed a child to construct a massive bridge over a plastic river, on which a tugboat towed a barge. Despite the creative efforts of the designers, when the LEGO System of Play went on sale in 1955 it met with only moderate success. "The Danish retail trade was skeptical," said GKC, "the German trade turned us down flat. The Germans didn't think they should import toys—from Denmark."

Once more, the company persevered in the face of sluggish sales: they made the LEGO system more complex and versatile, and improved the LEGO brick itself. Eventually, as GKC tells it, "the r-e-a-l, the final LEGO brick saw the light of day in 1958. That was when we invented the brick with the studs on top and tubes on the inside underneath. It was the tubes that gave the product its versatility and building stability. Suddenly it became possible to stack two eight-stud bricks [of the same color] in twenty-four different ways. Three bricks give you 1,060 ways!"

In 1958 the company began selling the new version of the brick—still in production today. Because the tightly joined bricks were more stable, it made possible more elaborate constructions. At the same time, the company began offering sloping bricks with which to make realistic roofs for buildings. As the company was introducing these improvements, Ole Kirk Christiansen died and leadership of the company passed to GKC.

50

In 1969 the DUPLO brick was introduced internationally for very young children. Double the size of a standard LEGO brick, a DUPLO brick is easy for a small child to handle and too large to be swallowed.

GKC understood that sales would continue to grow only if the product was constantly improved and renewed by fresh ideas. Through the 1960s the company's creative teams devised new elements and sets to make the LEGO system ever more versatile and appealing to children. In 1961 the company reinvented the wheel, LEGO-style, thus giving motility to the LEGO brick. In 1966 the first LEGO train rolled out; and three years later the company launched the DUPLO line of toys for small children. (The name DUPLO was derived from the fact that the basic DUPLO brick, in all its dimensions, was double the size of the basic LEGO brick, making it easier for little hands to grasp.) The 1960s saw such great success for the line that by 1970 one of the company's main problems was deciding how best to control its expanding market and manage it properly.

The introduction of wheels in 1962 added versatility to the system, allowing children to devise not only cars and trucks but any type of mobile creation they like. One idea that occurs to children all over the world is to put wheels on their LEGO brick animals, creating cats, elephants, even chickens on wheels.

In 1973 GKC's son, Kjeld Kirk Kristiansen, (his name was written with a "K" on his birth certificate, so he has kept that spelling) joined the LEGO company's managerial ranks after earning business degrees in Denmark and Switzerland. Kjeld's training, however, had begun almost thirty years earlier, when he and his two sisters used to test new LEGO toys for their play value before they went on the market, posing with them for the photographs on the boxes, and discussing them with their father. "I have always liked working with the product," Kjeld says, "and in fact I feel that I grew up together with it."

In 1973, when he officially started with the company, Kjeld's first projects were to participate in the establishment of manufacturing facilities in Switzerland and a technical research-and-development department that would keep the company's manufacturing methods up to date. He also aided in setting up LEGO Systems, Inc., the company's American manufacturing and sales operation, and helped reorganize the burgeoning LEGO product lines. By the end of the decade Kjeld had been named president of the company, thus assuring continued family control of the LEGO company. Kjeld also reaffirmed the company's commitment to producing only one thing, the LEGO System of Play, and doing it well—an "all-the-eggs-in-one-basket" philosophy that defies conventional corporate wisdom.

In a period of intense creative activity in the company, Kjeld emerged as the driving force behind marketing efforts and product development. Under his direction, the product development staff created a series of new items for the broadening spectrum of LEGO fans—dollhouses, baby rattles, ships, the TECHNIC line (As Technical as the Real Thing), and space models. However varied the product line became, every new item always had to be an integral part of the total LEGO system.

54

One of the most ingenious creations of the company's designers is the TECHNIC system, which came on the market in 1977. The great variety of gears, wheels, pulleys, and pumps—some of which are shown on the opposite page—enables children to create mechanical models that function realistically. With battery-powered TECHNIC motors, children can set their inventions in motion.

A System of Play

The LEGO system is not just a theory, but a practical program for creating toys with the greatest value for children. The fact that all pieces in the system are compatible means that a child who has four LEGO sets can use them all together to create more complex and interesting playthings than he could with four sets that didn't work together. In addition, the designers are always looking for ways to increase the system's "play value"—as if play value were a stock index that had to go up every year.

Play value is what a child can do with LEGO toys. When a new element creates new uses for old LEGO pieces, the play value of the system increases. Take the turntable, an element in the TECHNIC line that has a base on which a circular piece revolves. With it a child can build things that turn or spin—windmills, carousels, and mobiles, for example; the addition of a single new piece has added a whole new dimension of movement to the entire LEGO system.

The system as a whole undergoes a major overhaul every year, with about one-third of the catalogue being changed by the deletion of some sets and the addition of sixty to ninety new sets a year. The goal is not change for its own sake, but the enhancement of play value. When a new DUPLO ferry was introduced in 1984, it was designed to link up with existing DUPLO train sets, so a child could build a complete land and sea transport system.

The LEGO system of building bricks and special pieces is a creation so large and complex that only a child (or a toy salesman) can comprehend it. In the United States, the system is displayed in its full glory in a showroom, unfortunately off-limits to children, in a Manhattan office building, The Toy Center of the USA, that houses most of the showrooms of the toy industry. The LEGO company's designers have set up displays

In this busy riverside scene a motorized bulldozer delivers building elements, a crane lifts beams, and trucks haul goods to market. A child can create a whole pageant of industry and transportation.

The LEGOLAND Town system includes everything needed to create a realistic airport: helicopter, airliner, baggage trucks, and control tower—everything but the congestion.

of the whole range of LEGO toys, beginning with the DUPLO product program and culminating in huge layouts of the LEGOLAND fantasy systems—Town, Castle, and Space—creating the illusion that you have stepped into a parallel universe constructed entirely of LEGO toys. The Town system display includes a six-story apartment building, a hospital, airport, gas station, firehouse, police station, and a score of other buildings, as well as trucks, cars, a train, helicopters, boats, and airplanes. Male and female mini-figures of doctors, police, cargo handlers, and pilots populate the town. At the airport, mini-travelers sit contentedly in waiting rooms, but across town a tense drama is enacted as little firemen fight a house fire, with the flames represented by transparent yellow bricks that flash on and off.

Across the aisle, the calendar flips back a few centuries to the Middle Ages. An army is laying siege to an enormous castle. Catapults and bows are trained on the battlements, but many of the defending knights have retired to the castle's banquet hall for a mid-battle feast.

The display of the extremely successful line of space-age fantasy toys represents the busy exploration of some distant planet with a harsh, cratered landscape. Exploration vehicles bristling with antennae roam about, and spacemen file into a cave to make contact with an alien being that sparkles and glows with LEGO lights.

The colors may not match and the roof may not be properly sloped, but to a child's eye this is definitely a house. The young builder is making up her plans as she goes along, guided only by her fancy.

Perhaps the most interesting sight in the showroom is not one of the fantasy panoramas, but a glass wall about six feet high and fifteen feet wide, on which are displayed some of the individual elements that make up the LEGO system. The pieces are mounted in no particular order, very much like the photograph on the jacket of this book: propellers, motorcycles, wheels of all kinds and sizes, rattles, rocket engines, cows, locomotives, flowers, signs, tracks, latticework, and bricks in more shapes and with more functions than can be described. Creating a toy universe that actually works has obviously been a gargantuan task, and when the LEGO universe is thus broken down to its tiniest parts, the indefatigable ingenuity of the designers is fully apparent.

The strength of the LEGO company is the remarkable ability of the designers to constantly renew the system. Product development is carried on in great secrecy because of the intense competitiveness of the toy

Overleaf: With the Castle system, children construct thrilling scenes from the age of knighthood and chivalry. This fortress bristles with bowmen and ax-wielding warriors prepared to defend their town against a besieging army.

industry—spying is not unknown. The work of LEGO Futura's research-and-development teams, comprising about one hundred and fifty people, is accomplished behind locked doors, and nearly all other LEGO employees are barred from the studios in Billund and Copenhagen. Even when a new product has been successfully launched, the company is reluctant to reveal the nature of the work that went into it. LEGO toy designs have been copied so many times that the company is fearful that their rejected ideas could turn up on store shelves to compete against them. In one case, however, the company has decided to tell the story of a new product—the line of DUPLO rattles that were introduced in 1983.

A new product takes two to three years to develop, and represents the work of a surprisingly large number of people in diverse specialties: technicians, artists, toolmakers, economists, market analysts, graphics designers, buyers, and packaging designers. The DUPLO line of toys had been designed for children as young as a year old, but market research revealed that most children did not receive their first DUPLO toys until they were about two. So the company addressed the question of creating a product that would establish them more firmly in the infant market, and made its decision to begin the search for the new line of infant toys in 1979. In keeping with the cloak-and-dagger atmosphere of secrecy, the task had a code name, Project Baby (not exactly the kind of code to throw spies off the trail), and a schedule of two to three years for its completion.

The question was, what kind of toy should it be? To find their answer, the product development staff embarked on some highly unusual market research that led them to a most unlikely place, the British Museum. They wanted to find out not only what people were buying today, but what toys have appealed to infants throughout history. One member of the development team recalled: "We took a trip across to London to have a look at what the shops were selling in the way of baby products [and] we spent hours at the British Museum, where they have on display two or three of the oldest-known baby rattles in the world. From about 2000 B.C.! Right from the start of our project we knew that the basic product had to be a rattle, although we were perfectly aware that we couldn't *invent* it. We were a few thousand years too late for that."

A rattle would seem to be a relatively simple object to design, but the LEGO company's standards are very particular. The first requirements were that the rattle had to stimulate the baby's senses of hearing, sight,

The apparently simple double-grip rattle, blissfully chewed upon by an infant, was the result of years of technical and market research. The figure in the rattle is a duck with eyeballs that roll (infants instinctively respond to moving eyes) and, in place of a belly, a ball that the baby can spin. On the advice of a panel of mothers, the designers added two handles for a baby to grasp. Studs at the top and openings at the bottom permit the rattle to be attached to a child's DUPLO or LEGO bricks later on.

and touch (appealing not just to the fingers, but to that equally important organ of infant touching, the mouth). Psychological researchers informed the project managers that babies are interested in rattles only from the age of three months to six or seven months, but that they go through several stages of sensory development in that short time; one rattle would not hold the baby's interest for four months—there had to be a line of different rattles in ascending order of complexity. A final requirement was that the rattles had to be designed with the studs and tubes to connect them to other toys in the LEGO system. And, of course, they had to be of the quality that LEGO toy customers had come to expect.

The project was given to the company's design group in Copenhagen, who prepared the first prototypes by late 1980. The market-research department showed these early models to groups of mothers in Copenhagen, New York, Paris, Hamburg, and London, and invited their expert comments. The researchers found that one of the things uppermost in the minds of mothers was cleanliness. The mothers were pleased that the rattles were to be made of plastic instead of wood because they would be easier to keep clean. They preferred the vivid LEGO colors to more subtle pastel shades, and they stood firm against any rattle that could be taken apart—a feature the designers had included to give the rattles additional play value and make them appealing to the inquisitive one-year-old as well as to the infant. What most surprised the researchers was the mothers' complaints that the prototypes (as well as most rattles already on the market) were too large and heavy for infants.

The group was faced with having to redesign their rattles almost completely, reducing their size and weight, and adding a new feature inspired by the mothers' comments—handles. The mothers had placed such emphasis on the ability of a child to hold a rattle easily that the designers furnished the rattles with a pair of handles that an infant could grip with both hands.

The new designs underwent more tests with psychologists, teachers, and the infants themselves, and then had to face the scrutiny of the product safety department for final approval. Before the rattles reached the market there was one last obstacle—some of the squeaking components ordered from an outside supplier didn't squeak, so every last one of them had to be squeezed by hand to make sure that it worked and that there would be no disappointed babies.

A preschooler's DUPLO brick forms the foundation for a fanciful assemblage created by the company's designers to demonstrate that virtually everything in the LEGO system fits together. A DUPLO girl sits atop a baby's rattle, while a bicycle-riding postman from a LEGOLAND Town set and an action figure from a TECHNIC set are poised over a window borrowed from a FABULAND set.

Precision in Plastic

Judging by its straightforward appearance, the LEGO brick would seem to be a simple object to manufacture. Actually, it is a precision-made item, the product of three decades of engineering. The essence of LEGO bricks is that they are easy to connect to one another, yet they stick together tenaciously until you pull them apart — and they stand up to this use for years. If you had ten- or twenty-year-old LEGO bricks they would fasten perfectly onto a brick you bought yesterday.

The property responsible for this high performance of the plastic brick is called "clutch power," the LEGO brick version of "stick-to-itiveness." Matt Ramsey, the British engineer who helped coordinate the design of the company's Enfield, Connecticut plant and is now vice-president of manufacturing, defines clutch power as "the pulling force you have to apply to pull two bricks apart. Clutch power has to maintain consistency for the life of the brick, which could be more than twenty years. That's why we use special materials and molding techniques." The same high standards of manufacture are maintained at all five of the company's brick-producing plants, located in the United States, Denmark, Switzerland, South Korea, and Brazil.

In order to hold together firmly the bricks have to be meticulously manufactured, and over the years the LEGO company has developed a manufacturing system devoted to creating a flawless product. The accuracy of their production is legendary in the toy industry. The "tolerance" — the allowable variation of the diameters of studs and tubes — is two-hundredths of a millimeter, about eight ten-thousandths of an inch. In order to attain this high degree of perfection, the LEGO company manufactures its own molds in three shops in Germany and Switzerland. Their engineers, over the years, have also modified the machines used to

One of the molds used at the Billund plant makes only eight bricks at a time, ensuring that quality can be precisely controlled.

In one of the molding halls at Billund an elaborate system of tubes carries plastic granules from the holding bins (above) to various molding machines.

produce plastic items, and developed their own specifications for the plastics used to create the bricks and other elements. Most LEGO elements are formed of a type of plastic known as ABS, for acrylonitrile butadiene styrene. Matt Ramsey claims that in the techniques of molding high-quality plastic items, the LEGO company leads the toy industry.

LEGO bricks, like many plastic objects, are made by the injection-molding process. At the Billund factory, rows and rows of molding machines stand in the hangar-like molding halls, covering about 7,250 square meters (almost 78,000 square feet) in all. There is a slight aroma of plastic in the air, but the floors are spotlessly clean, and no tools or loose equipment can be seen lying around. A network of steel tubing runs overhead, with branches descending to each machine. These tubes carry the raw granules of plastic from holding bins in another part of the factory. This hall of robotic machines is run by only a few humans—the molding process is so automated that only a handful of workers is needed to monitor the machines.

Atop each molding machine is a glassed-in compartment where the little drama of LEGO brick creation takes place amid the clanking of molds and the wheeze of hydraulics. The raw plastic granules—yellow, red, blue, black, grey, or white—are funneled into a tube, and heat is applied. The heat and the pressure soften the plastic, raising its temperature to about 450 degrees Fahrenheit. The hot plastic, with the consistency of paste, is then injected into the mold, which is kept at about 85 degrees. Under pressure varying from twenty-four to one hundred and fifty tons, depending on the piece, the bricks are molded into shape.

The few seconds the plastic spends inside the mold are crucial to its quality—if the temperature and pressure are not maintained precisely, the pieces will be defective or weak. The company's engineers designed a cooling system to keep the molds within one degree of the required temperature and a hydraulic system to maintain the great pressure needed. The entire molding hall has to be climate-controlled, partly

because ABS absorbs moisture. The plastic granules are run through a dryer before reaching the molding machines, and the relative humidity in the hall itself is maintained at 50%.

Another factor contributing to the high quality of the bricks is the small capacity of the LEGO mold. Many plastics manufacturers use molds that can spit out sixty units per cycle. The LEGO company uses much smaller molds, in order to maintain greater consistency and control over quality, although at a very high cost. A mold, fashioned of hardened steel and polished to a high sheen with diamond dust, eventually wears out from the heat, pressure, and friction of the plastic, and its replacement cost is in the tens of thousands of dollars.

When the "curing" of the bricks is finished, the mold automatically opens, and a robot arm reaches down to grab the length of excess plastic that has been extruded. The bricks fall into a cardboard box below, and the robot tosses the extra plastic, called the runner, into a bin, from which

71

A worker pours components into a counting machine. Electronic machines in the assembly shop (above) put together small components. Some elements are welded together ultrasonically.

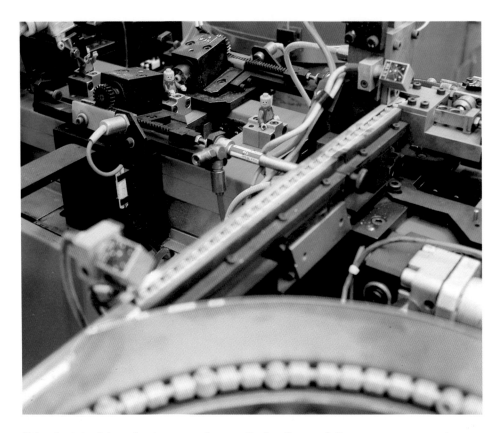

it is shunted to a hopper and recycled—the molding process wastes no plastic. Every few seconds, the box under each machine begins to rock back and forth as an automatic agitator shakes it so that the bricks will settle evenly At any given moment, dozens of these agitators may be at work, tossing thousands of LEGO bricks and creating an unearthly rustling sound. The molding machines count the number of pieces they produce, and when a certain point is reached the machine knows that the box is full. Automatically, the full box is shunted aside and an empty box slides into its place.

The company takes extraordinary measures to ensure that no defective bricks find their way to the consumer. The injection-molding machines are equipped with built-in monitors to detect fluctuations in temperature and pressure. A malfunction automatically sets off an alarm. The machines are also able to detect some types of brick deformation and shunt those pieces aside, but other defects are too subtle to be detected by the injection machines, so a human eye is needed. The workers in charge of the machines watch for mistakes, but the guardian

A product-safety engineer tests a batch of DUPLO figures, designed for small children, to make certain that the heads cannot be pulled off too easily. Testing by hand is not sufficiently exact—the engineer uses a machine that tugs at the toys with a preset, unvarying force.

of quality at the plants is the quality-control technician, who makes a systematic tour of all the molding machines and scoops up a sampling of their output. These are taken back to the inspection station, where the technician dumps the bricks on a table and examines them piece by piece for variations in color tone or in the thickness of the plastic, malformed studs, and something called a "high gate," an excess of plastic at the point where the plastic was injected into the mold. Bricks that seem perfectly acceptable to an outsider are sternly rejected. The technician pulled a previously rejected brick from a drawer and held it up to the light. The brick was apparently flawless but on close examination the light shone through it at one tiny spot—an unacceptable variation. The quality-control technician is an authority unto himself, with the power to halt the production line, if necessary, any time the bricks are less than perfect.

The factories in Billund, Denmark and Baar, Switzerland are equipped with assembly shops and decoration shops to produce items with multiple parts and painted decorations. Assembly is done both by hand and by machine. Human hands put together battery units and doll's-house cupboards, but automatic assembly machines are used to assemble such items as wheel units and miniature human figures. In the process of a BASIC figure's mechanical birth, a machine inserts heads into torsos, and then the little beings-in-the-making are guided along chutes to a painting machine that imprints eyes, noses, and winning smiles.

A prepacking line automatically shunts the required number of elements into small bags, which will later be placed in boxes. Sensitive computer-controlled counting and weighing devices, and many pairs of vigilant human eyes, have virtually eliminated packing errors.

The task of packing bricks, construction elements, and other items is extremely complex. Like the molding process, packing is automated, but the human factor is also crucial to the high quality the company achieves in its packaging. The packing operators, some sitting by conveyor belts that deliver bags of pieces to work stations, and others sitting at large tables, dexterously fold boxes, nestle pieces into their proper niches, and constantly keep an eye out for errors that escaped the mechanical sensors of the machines.

The automated portion of the packing process is fascinating to watch—an intricately choreographed mechanical dance. Pieces are bagged on "pre-pack" lines, which are basically conveyor belts. Each line is about thirty-six feet long, with sixteen bins stationed along it, holding different elements. Small boxes, called cassettes, move along the belt under the bins, from which the requisite number of bricks drops into each passing cassette. The LEGO system of toys includes hundreds of different sets; an individual set might have anywhere from a dozen bricks in its box to more than three hundred. Counting and packing these pieces mechanically is an immensely complicated problem, for which the company devised typically ingenious solutions of which they are justifiably proud. Matt Ramsey remarked that "if you go to other manufacturers, you often find a bunch of people counting bits into a box." With its abhorrence of error and its zest for efficiency, the LEGO company worked for years to create a virtually failureproof packing and checking system. The company, says Ramsey, "invested a great deal of money" to defeat what he refers to darkly as "the Problem of the Missing Piece."

Overleaf: Packers deftly fold boxes into shape and fill them with bags of pieces and instruction booklets. Before the boxes are finally sealed, they are checked by machine to make certain that no pieces are missing from the set.

A toy designed for preschool children must meet rigorous standards: its size must be tested to ensure that it is too large to be swallowed by a three-year-old, and its material must be strong enough to withstand a simulated bite.

Perfection in molding and packing is secondary to one other concern—product safety. LEGO toys, of course, must conform to all the safety regulations imposed by the various countries where they are sold. The toys have to withstand drop tests, twisting tests, and biting tests (performed by machines that duplicate the human bite, not by test children). The purpose of these tests is to ensure that no piece can be broken apart and then swallowed. The materials also have to be tested for toxicity.

In the 1970s there was a controversy in Denmark, Great Britain, and Sweden over cadmium, a heavy metal that the human body cannot excrete, contained in the color pigments for the yellow and red LEGO bricks, as well as in products made by other companies. The LEGO company was able to demonstrate that there was no way for the cadmium to leach out of its products, and even if it did, the amount of cadmium present was far too small to do any harm to children. But aside from the health issue, an environmental concern was raised—discarded plastic toys would remain in landfills for centuries, during which time the cadmium could leach out and pollute water supplies. The company then decided to change the specifications for its plastic so that it would be cadmium-free—a costly decision, because the absence of cadmium made the molding process more difficult.

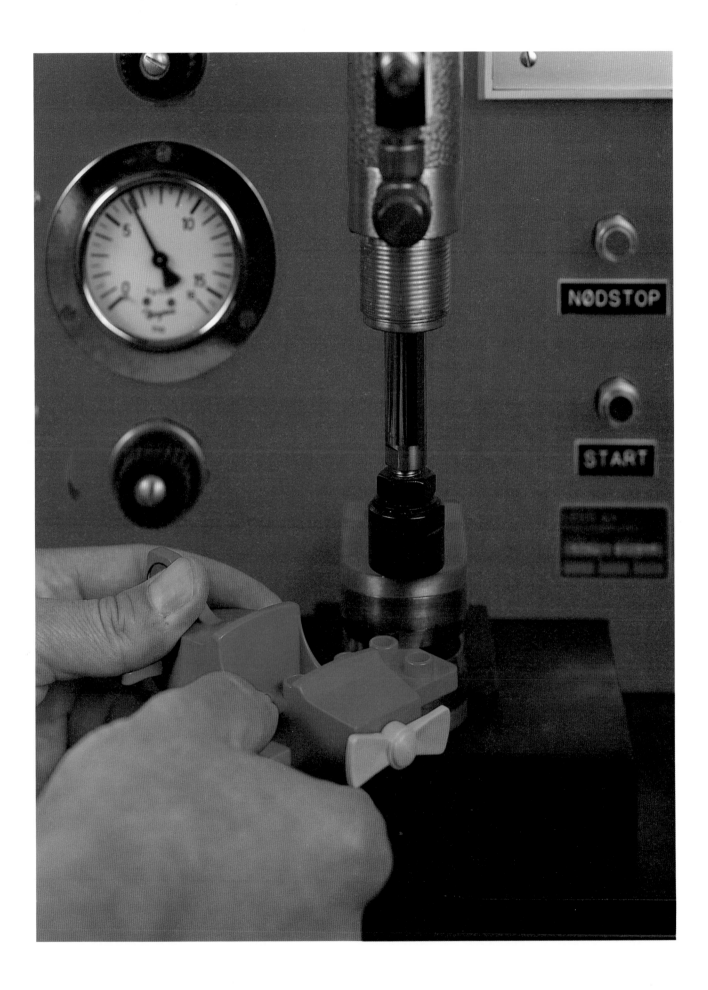

The Theory of a Toy

In 1980 the LEGO company published a book of essays about play, creativity, and education with a title that neatly encapsulates their philosophy of the uses of play—*Serious Fun*. That paradoxical concept, that fun is fun, but it is also important, is the foundation of the company's approach to toy making. (It is tempting to call it the Tao of LEGO.) The department responsible for developing new LEGO products for children is not called Product Development, but LEGO Futura, which can be taken to mean The Future of the LEGO Way. The man in charge of developing books and films in the publishing department of LEGO Futura, until his death in 1986, was an avuncular Dane, bearded and slightly built, named Olaf Thygesen Damm. With twenty-five years of experience at the company, he had become the in-house philosopher of the LEGO system, the LEGO theory, and the LEGO idea. A visitor taken to see Olaf Damm would be told that he was about to get "the LEGO Infusion."

When he spoke of the LEGO system and the rarified "pure LEGO idea," Damm assumed the postures and tones of a philosopher, one who had pondered the nature of childhood and knew that the answers to its deeper questions might always elude him. When asked about the reasons for LEGO toys' remarkable appeal to children he responded: "Why have we become so successful? Who can know the complete truth?" And then he launched into "the LEGO Infusion."

"If we look at the pure LEGO idea—what is LEGO? It is a various number of components in different shapes and colors, with the possibility of combining them in many, many ways. There is no end to the combinations. What we are really giving children are opportunities to be active in a meaningful way—this is the basic idea."

In building a complex model by following the instructions, a child learns to think methodically and to tackle difficult tasks one step at a time.

And then he turned the question around from the product's success to its appeal: "It is more interesting to ask, why are children so interested in building with LEGO bricks? Most toys have a short lifetime. What makes children come back to the LEGO toy day after day, year after year? It starts with what children are, and what their projects are. Children need to be active. You will never see healthy passive children. A healthy child is always looking for something interesting to do. When such children come to a new place they say, 'What can I use here, what is here for me? ' They find and investigate. They want to use their own resources.

"It is important that the material they get in their hands is not finished, not ready-made. The bricks invite the children to be active, to do something, they *call for* activity. The various possibilities are endless. Most toys are empty of new possibilities. With LEGO bricks one can always find something new to do. The activity is engaging, fun, absorbing, challenging, rewarding.

"Play is the dominating activity of children, as work is the dominating activity of grown-ups. Play is very important, because in play children use their senses, their brain, imagination, social ability—all kinds of resources are activated in the play process. Play is for the most part undisciplined, free, voluntary, and it is *fun*, and we should never forget that. We can tend to take toys so seriously that we can forget that play must be fun. Otherwise it's not play. Children's play and grown-ups' work are very different.

83

Toys give form to a child's fantasies, bring-
ing daydreams to life. This boy can spend
hours acting out his imaginary medieval
adventures.

"Children have an innate need for development. We see, even when children are very small, how eager they are to involve themselves in the world. They investigate, they experiment, they try things out, and they use all their resources very eagerly. It comes from inside. It's a demanding process to be a child, to try to fit into society. There are many conflicts, many problems to solve, many defeats on the way to becoming a grown-up. It's a very hard time. Children need tools for their creative play; what we call toys could be called tools for play. And the better children play, the better they will master the world."

As a tool for creative play, the LEGO brick has few equals. The simplicity of its design allows children to do just about anything they want, at whatever level of challenge suits them. A child can decide to make his project as simple or as complex as he wishes. LEGO toys are never so easy that they are boring, or so difficult to work with that they are frustrating.

84

Using only four pieces, a three-year-old girl created a smiling man on a bridge. An eight-year-old girl's creation was more elaborate—she imagined herself as the driver of this delightful car, with a roof that swings back and forth depending on the weather.

1 2

2 × 6   **6 × 2**

3 × 4   **4 × 3**

LEGO Bricks in the Classroom

From the time that the LEGO company first introduced its system of play, one of the principles of its philosophy was that toys should help children to develop in a sound and healthy way. By the late 1960s, teachers all over Europe had recognized the educational value of LEGO toys and were using them in the classroom as teaching aids. In 1980 the company decided to establish a special department to refine the educational concepts behind their toys, and to develop toys specifically for classroom use.

Teachers had brought LEGO toys into the classroom for a number of reasons, which varied depending upon the age level of the children in the class. For one thing, there was a growing awareness among teachers that book learning tended to make children passive absorbers of information, and should be supplemented with more active methods of learning information and skills. Teachers were also concerned that an emphasis on reading skills would do little to foster a child's total physical and mental development. As the Italian educator Loris Malaguzzi wrote: "A child has one hundred languages but is robbed of ninety-nine. School and civilization separate the head from the body. They take away one vital form of contact with the senses. They force one to think without the body. . . . Play and work, reality and imagination . . . are forced to become opposites."

Children learn the basics of arithmetic by moving colorful blocks on a board. They can more easily grasp the concept of multiplication when they see "6 x 2" represented by two rows of six bricks.

Realistic technical components from LEGO sets allow students to learn mechanical principles with relative ease. Using bricks, students build simple devices such as those on the right, illustrating the principles of cantilevering and balance.

No one was suggesting that the classroom be turned into a playroom, but educators were beginning to realize that toys could serve a very useful educational purpose. To accept that idea, a teacher or parent had to have some faith in the judgment of children, and to redefine their idea of play. A former Minister of Education in Denmark, K. Helveg Petersen, wrote that "children by and large opt for things . . . that offer a challenge and demand the application of imagination, thought, and constructive skills. This makes play much more than a pastime; it becomes instruction, learning, enrichment, and human development."

Many adults, because of the old Puritan beliefs that nothing is good for you if it doesn't hurt a bit, that education needs some force behind it, tend to resist the idea that much can be learned through certain kinds of

play. We forget that doing something just because one wants to do it can be a very strong force for motivating a child. If toys stimulate creative activity, and the children like playing with toys, what could be the harm? Many parents remain unconvinced. One Danish teacher wrote: "The parental complaint is often, 'They're not at school to play, but to learn.' My usual reply is, 'Exactly.'"

Adults often do not realize that some very simple concepts—big versus small, many versus few, high versus low, and the differences between colors—are new ideas to very young children, ideas that have to be learned and refined. Playing with brightly colored bricks gives children the chance to learn these concepts through a pleasant experience. DU-PLO bricks are very useful in helping preschool children learn to recognize different shapes and colors: they learn how to match objects according to colors, and to create patterns out of bricks in different colors, sizes, and shapes. Physical development can also be aided by play: merely pressing the bricks together and pulling them apart helps children acquire dexterity and develop eye–hand coordination.

Language and social skills develop when a group of children play together with bricks. Building a model requires each child to identify the pieces needed by size and color, and then to get them from a classmate without an argument. The child soon learns how to persuade another child that it is a good idea for him to use the yellow bricks and give up the blue ones. Simple addition and subtraction are learned through experience, as the builder of a half-finished red car totes up the number of red pieces left in his box and asks himself, "How many more red bricks will I need to finish this car?"

Play is a powerful aid to conceptual development. For example, making a model by copying a photograph shows the children that a two-dimensional photograph stands for something real, and that it can be converted into a three-dimensional object. The powers of memory develop as children learn to recall what they have built from one day to the next; they gradually learn to remember more details—how large yesterday's house was, what color it was, and how many windows it had. Completing a relatively complicated model might take sixty to ninety minutes—an enormous span of time for a child—which teaches the child to approach a task on a step-by-step basis and to concentrate for an extended period. Gradually attention span increases. The child also attains self-confidence when he or she has successfully completed a model.

In late preschool and early primary school, teachers begin to use LEGO theme sets that give children the chance to build such things as farms, harbors, or gas stations—places and things they recognize from the real world. The children build these things not only for the experience of building them, but in order to play at operating them. It helps the children gain a deeper understanding of the way the world works. When they have built a farm, for example, it naturally leads the teacher to ask, "What does a cow do? Is that where we get milk? What are the men doing in the barn?" And the discussion of cows and milk leads to talk about food in general, about what foods are good to eat, and where food comes

The elegant number display, designed to look like a ladder, graphically illustrates the principles of addition and subtraction and is used to teach simple arithmetic.

90

Children are surprisingly eager to learn about complicated mechanical principles when they can build examples with their own hands.

Classroom science projects include assembling a simple lever, which demonstrates how different weights can be kept in balance. One piece positioned at the end of the lever can support the weight of two other pieces attached closer to the fulcrum on the opposite side.

from. The sets also encourage children to make up stories about what they have built, stimulating creativity. With concrete material the children get interested in subjects they might otherwise find abstract and boring.

The different levels of LEGO toys are designed to suit the needs of children at particular stages of development. An infant does not play in a systematic way, but uses his senses and his muscles. If you give a baby a rattle he will turn it, twist it, listen to the sound it makes, taste it, and throw it aside. Older children learn to pretend with toys, and almost anything can become a toy. A stick, lifted into the air, becomes a jet plane.

Role playing, the imitation of adults, leads children to pretending that they are policemen, doctors, mothers, or fathers. Role playing is especially important to a child's development between the ages of five and seven. At this stage, children like to copy the activities of adults—driving, cooking, shopping, cleaning. They adopt the roles of people they see every day—a shopkeeper, teacher, parent, or bus driver—and act out imaginary situations and events, or, to the embarrassment of adults, reenact private dramas they have witnessed. This type of role

A machine that turns a wheel when it is cranked shows the workings of a drive chain. The gear attached to a rod keeps the chain taut. A child who has constructed this machine could design a motorized truck with a similar system.

playing can be important psychologically because in "pretend" games the child is free to act out feelings normally hidden—anger, fear, jealousy—which the child senses the parents would find unacceptable.

Through role playing, children learn to act in the world. They learn about themselves by trying on the roles of others in different relationships. A child's way of making sense out of the world is to convert it to a game. Children, while observing plenty, prefer to be active participants; since they cannot really drive a car or deliver the mail, they play that they can. They learn social skills—one child is the driver, and the other is the passenger. Or one writes the letter, the other delivers it. Children like to use dolls, cars, toy houses, boats, and animals to help them act their roles, because toys add an element of reality to the imagined stories.

Teachers have found that shy children enjoy working with LEGO toys, and learn to express themselves more easily behind the shield of playthings. Children who are retarded or have mental disorders often spurn any contact with a teacher, but the smooth, brightly colored DUPLO bricks are so attractive that even inaccessible children are eager to

Although the LEGO system features carefully designed models of all kinds, the sets also foster free-form playing. When left on their own with a pile of bricks, children will instinctively start to build towers. The very tall towers that set world records, however, utilize special construction techniques involving adhesives.

handle them, and are more likely to establish contact with a teacher. Such children don't usually attempt complicated building projects; they like to arrange the bricks by colors or build the highest towers they can—a simple building activity gives them real motivation. The bricks can also serve as a means of getting parents to interact with their disabled children. Parents are accustomed to leaving their kids alone with their toys, but therapists try to get parents to play together with their disabled children, establishing a closer relationship.

Blind children derive many benefits from playing with bricks. They learn, by feel, to distinguish different shapes and dimensions; they learn the shapes of houses, animals, and vehicles by actually building them, and, because the bricks can be fastened together so easily, the children gain confidence from building ever more complex models.

LEGO toys also open up the world of technology to children. The TECHNIC line of building sets, with which children can make complex and realistic mechanical devices, is designed for children from the age of seven to twelve, to develop their understanding of basic scientific and mechanical principles. Children start off by learning to identify and classify different pieces—what is a gear? What different kinds and sizes of gears are there? They learn to build a simple rectangular structure and stabilize it; they find out what makes a structure apt to collapse under a weight. Simple experiments with friction demonstrate how difficult it can be to move an object without mechanical assistance, and then they progress to building a little conveyor belt out of LEGO bricks, gears, and elastic bands.

When imagination is given free rein, creative play can be therapeutic. An eleven-year-old girl made a yellow dog with fierce red eyes and a long tail. He is carefully fenced in by a rectangle of bricks. The combination of car and helicopter was designed by an eleven-year-old boy who clearly likes big, powerful machines.

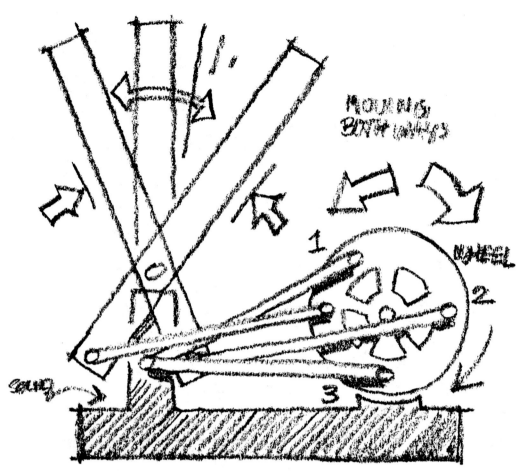

Instead of studying drawings and photos of how things work, children can actually build things themselves and discover the secret of their operation.

A few experiments with gears reveal secrets of the mechanical world that many adults do not even understand. The children discover that meshing a small gear to a larger one slows down the speed of a mechanism, but increases its power. They find that adding a pulley to a crane allows them to lift a much greater weight than if they use a gear all by itself. Once they've grasped the basic principle behind gears—that they serve to transmit motion from one part of a machine to another—the children can start using the more advanced TECHNIC sets that reproduce machines from real life—drills, cars, ratchets, washing machines, cranes, and clocks. Machines that had been a mystery become comprehensible, and the children find out that some of the most complex devices in real life are based on simple mechanical principles. They find out how machines lift, steer, and use wind and water as sources of power.

A mechanical concept that intrigues children is the transformation of one type of motion into another. In this machine the circular motion of the gear is changed into the back-and-forth movement of the lever.

Perhaps most important of all (and least understood), working with LEGO bricks is training in thinking—methodical thinking, which proceeds from the step-by-step building of a LEGO model, and creative thinking, which occurs when a child tosses the instructions aside and strikes out on his own.

Many children and adults simply do not know how to think. They do not know how to analyze a problem in a way that will make it more manageable, and when they are confronted with an unfamiliar situation, for which they have no training or experience, they are at a loss. In an interview he conducted with himself for the book *Serious Fun*, Edward de Bono, Director of the Centre for Thinking at Cambridge University, discussed how ways of thinking can result in creativity: "The great insights of thinking arrive from looking at something which has been done in one way and suddenly realizing that it can be done in a better or simpler way." He also described "the joy of playing around. You set out to move things about and to build them up and you don't quite know what you are going to do, but as you go along, something suggests itself out of what you have already got. This sort of creative exploration is an extremely important part of thinking. . . . It teaches us how to explore, it teaches us how to be curious, it teaches us how to build on. Far too many adults lack this ability to play around and 'see what happens.'"

One of the first concepts students learn when they begin to work with LEGO technical sets is how to brace a structure to make it stable. Once they have mastered this simple idea, children use girders to build tall sturdy towers.

Combining small and large gears affects the speed and strength of a mechanical device. This machine has six gears, but children like to assemble complex inventions with dozens of gears for the pure joy of seeing all of them turning at the same time.

98

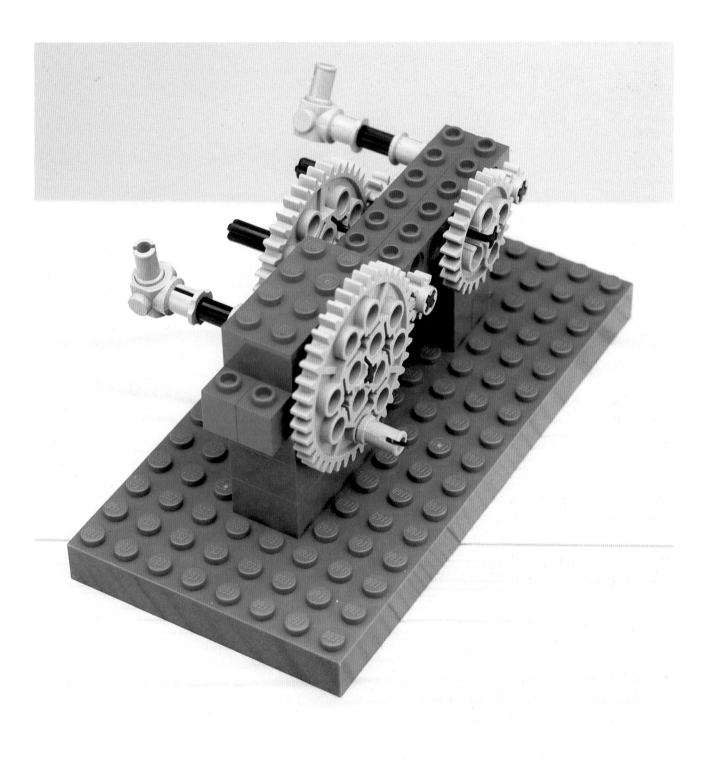

The Brick Meets the Computer

The LEGO system's impact on children's thinking patterns was one of the factors that brought the LEGO company into an alliance with another system for thinking—the computer. For the European educational market the company has developed a system, called TECHNIC CONTROL, that allows students to write their own computer programs to control motorized models, such as an automatic sliding door, a washing machine, a robot arm, and a "plotter" that draws multicolored geometric patterns on a sheet of paper. The system, intended for students aged eleven to fourteen, teaches basic concepts of mechanics and computer operation, while at the same time encouraging methodical thinking. In completing a project, the students learn the interrelationship between designing the physical structure of a model, designing its mechanical components, and writing a computer program to run the model.

Experiments with younger students have also been proceeding in the United States, where a remarkable pilot project is underway at the Hennigan School, a public school in Boston, Massachusetts. It is sponsored by the LEGO company and carried out under the guidance of education and computer specialists from the Massachusetts Institute of Technology.

A visitor to the Hennigan classroom while the project was in full swing might have thought that the students were having a play period. In groups of three or four, the sixteen fifth-graders were building houses, trucks, and other structures of indeterminate shapes and purposes, from bins full of LEGO bricks. LEGO brick cars zipped along the floor, pursued by their laughing designers. Instructors moved from group to group, giving advice and answering questions, but for the most part the children seemed to be on their own, making whatever LEGO con-

The company has recently designed a line of educational models that can be programmed with computers using the Logo computer language. Children write their own programs to control LEGO models, including cars, miniature appliances, and toys they have invented themselves.

structions came into their heads. Some were rolling their cars down a ramp; others plugged their motorized models into a power box and intently watched the cars go through their paces.

Amidst all this apparently aimless play, it came as a surprise to see that the power boxes running these toys were connected to a pair of computers. Even more surprising, every now and then one of the students stepped up to a computer, tapped in a few lines of commands, and then watched the vehicle react. The children were indeed playing, but they were simultaneously learning to program a computer, to build LEGO brick structures according to basic mechanical principles, and, perhaps most important, they were learning how to learn.

The intellectual eminence behind the project is Seymour Papert, professor of mathematics and education at MIT and the cofounder of MIT's Artificial Intelligence Laboratory. In the 1970s he developed Logo, an easy-to-learn, yet powerful computer language, which the Hennigan students are using to program their LEGO brick constructions. Papert simplified the task of programming a computer to the point where children as young as eight could perform interesting tasks. In his book *Mindstorms* Papert described how computers can revolutionize learning, not only by teaching children mathematics and computing, but by teaching them to think systematically and to solve problems in an organized way.

The LEGO company, already in the midst of developing LEGO LINES, was intrigued by Papert's work with children. They got in touch with him in 1984. Together they embarked upon the pilot project at the Hennigan School, with an eye toward introducing a computer-driven LEGO product for primary schools in the United States. Linked with LEGO bricks, the computer becomes an extremely effective tool for teaching young children, as the faculty and students at Hennigan discovered.

Ten-year-old Nicky was hunched over a worktable, earnestly fitting and refitting sensors and wires into a complex contraption of his own design. When he had finished his machine—about eight inches long; six wide; and five high—it looked as if it would be able to perform several functions at once. On one side there was a conveyor belt, made out of LEGO tractor treads, with a single LEGO brick attached on top of it. On the other side, not yet put into place, was a wall of yellow bricks with a dozen or so interlocking gears, left over from a LEGO brick counting device Nicky had made. He was installing a light sensor at one end of the conveyor belt, and a touch sensor at the other end. Somehow a tiny motorized vehicle, which Nicky identified as a tank, had a role in this apparatus.

The wires from the sensors and the motors will be plugged into a computer. Nicky's device will gather data, automatically feed it into the computer, and then respond to instructions from the computer. Using Logo, Nicky had partially written his own program to operate his device. When asked to describe what his machine will do, Nicky immediately launched into a detailed explanation: "The computer will tell this motor to turn this block [on the conveyor belt] one of these ways. If it goes to the left, it's going to cut off the light to this sensor, which will tell the computer to turn it around. And then it will turn around and hit this touch sensor, which will tell the computer . . . I'm not sure what will happen then, but I was thinking it could either make this tank move, or . . . I'm going to put a lot of gears and stuff here, so it could make all these gears move. I'm not sure how I'm going to do it, but I can probably manage," he said confidently.

The children in the program were not chosen exclusively from among the brightest; in fact, some had learning difficulties and reading-related problems. The purpose of the program is not to create a fast track of future computer geniuses, but to demonstrate the capability of computers and LEGO bricks to stimulate the learning capacities of all children, particularly the slower ones. The LEGO company and Professor Papert have long believed that children with learning problems can be the ones to benefit most from creative play.

In the pilot project the children worked with the computer and the LEGO bricks for four weeks. They started out building simple cars, which they rolled down a cardboard ramp. Each child measured the distance his or her car traveled, and then got to work modifying the design to make it go farther. (Interestingly, the children quickly forgot that distance was what they were measuring and began to think in terms of speed—a more enjoyable form of measurement.)

Working with motors led the children to experiments with gears, pulleys, and other devices for transmitting power from a motor, concepts that they found fascinating. They grasped the idea of gear ratio right away. One girl, who built a car that goes very slowly, explained that its sedate speed was caused by the meshing of a large gear and a small one: "This gear turns this one, and when the first one turns three times this one turns just once—three turns of this one make one turn of that one." (One of the most provocative findings of the pilot project has been that girls, contrary to what much educational research has shown, can be as interested as boys in "technical" things such as gears, computers, and complex LEGO building sets.)

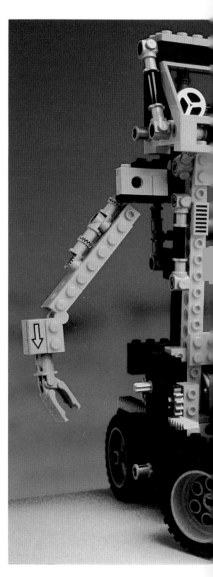

The versatility of the LEGO system makes it the perfect companion for a computer—there is almost no limit to the kinds of device that can be built with LEGO bricks and programmed on a computer. It is quite simple to program a computer to turn a motor on and off at specified times, and to instruct the motor to reverse direction; so a car can be programmed to run for five seconds, stop, run backwards for ten seconds, and then repeat the process. Simple programs and machines can be made far more complex and interesting by the addition of sensors that detect light or contact with an object. A car, equipped with sensors that react to touch at the front and back, can be programmed to turn or reverse direction whenever it bumps into something.

One of the students' assignments was to think of the house of the future, and design things that might be in it. One group designed an automatic elevator with a touch sensor at the top that detected when the elevator had reached the roof, and sent it back down again. Another group built a toaster with a computerized timer so that light or dark toast could be preselected. Their kitchen of the future had a stove with lights for burners and for the oven element. The children programmed the lights to turn on for various periods of time to "cook" different foods.

The fact that the children could use LEGO bricks to create models of real-life objects was what fired their imaginations. As Papert said, "They're able to draw on the tremendous expertise and the passion they

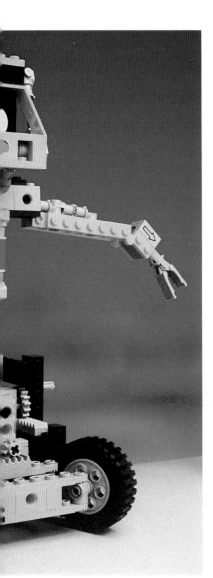

have for these constructions, and their interest in cars or kitchens or homes or machines—all this unites with the activity with the computer in a kind of chemical mix. What comes out is a formal knowledge of the mathematics of programming, and the scientific ideas embedded in using the computer, always rooted in and fueled by the child's contact with the real world and the child's passion for the activities of real life."

The children's imaginations roamed beyond the things of real life to create fanciful constructions—LEGO brick devices that sprang from a pure love of mechanical creation. Nicky designed a clever vehicle he called "The Walker," which was inspired by an observation he made while working with LEGO electric motors. He noticed that when a motor runs it produces vibrations, and wondered if a model could be made to move purely by the strength of vibration. He placed a motor on a platform, and supported it on four stilts. When he turned on the Walker it did not perform very well, but he had a further idea. To increase the strength of the vibrations he put a gear in front of the motor, attached another gear to it with a loop of LEGO chain, and inserted a stick into the second gear. Nicky didn't know it, but his double gear-and-chain mechanism embodied the principle of the ball joint.

When the motor was turned on, the pole at the front spun around, off-balance, and made the Walker jump around; but Nicky was still not satisfied. Another boy, observing Nicky's work, had the idea of attaching wheels to the Walker's stilts—but not in the expected way. Instead of putting the wheels on axles, he and Nicky attached them horizontally, so the wheels looked like round rubber feet. Now the Walker performed beautifully, zipping around in circles, with its front stick whirling like some kind of weird snout.

In the traditional classroom, children learn that copying another student's work is one of the cardinal sins. But in the Hennigan project the children were encouraged to learn from each other's work, and to take an idea a step further. The instructors and observers have noted that new ideas spread quickly throughout the class. Stephen Ocko, an associate of Papert who has been working closely with the teachers and students at Hennigan, noticed that "when ideas like the vibrating Walker come into this world, the children pick them up and elaborate on them. There are many, many vibrating devices that were inspired by the Walker—all of them different."

This motorized robot on wheels, with movable arms and rack-and-pinion steering, is an example of a toy which a child can build with LEGO elements and program with Logo.

The children come to expect that creative things will happen when they are working with the LEGO bricks. They learn to look for the "side effects"—Ocko's phrase for the serendipitous things the children discover as they work. Many of the children's inspirations grew out of a scarcity of pieces. In the early weeks of the pilot program, the class had an enormous supply of bricks to work with, but the instructors reduced the supply to see if the students could work with the more limited selection of bricks contained in the sets eventually put on the market. An education specialist who spent several months observing the project believed that the students would not be able to work as well with the reduced supply, but the children proved to be more resourceful than she predicted. "They invented the most ingenious solutions because of the scarcity. They didn't have enough wheels, yet they made all these cars—it was incredible! For wheels they used gears and dial faces—anything that was round."

Ocko noted that, in the economy of scarcity, "interesting things happen—one, the children are forced to look for the essence of the design, so what you see are structures designed in a very simple and elegant way. It can't be too elaborate: they have to look for the most economical way. The other thing is an interesting social interaction, because they have to work out trades, and sharing. We're seeing extraordinary teamwork and cooperation. It's a very exciting environment."

Adding excitement to the classroom was one of the primary goals of the project, because Papert believes that the atmosphere of the traditional classroom has inhibited learning. In a magazine interview he said, "For many children, traditional school is a very dangerous place because you can be humiliated, embarrassed—scared [it will be] found out that you don't know how to do something."

He pointed out that children have an innately positive attitude toward learning: they spontaneously learn words, for example. But he believes that many children have been inhibited in their learning because our method of teaching is based on "right" answers and "wrong" answers. Children are often taught that there is only one right answer to a question, and they soon find out that the student who consistently comes up with wrong answers is a failure. This approach may work for teaching the names of continents and countries, but it does not teach children how to solve problems.

Seymour Papert, a professor at the Massachusetts Institute of Technology and a noted authority on computer languages, has shown that students labeled as slow learners can improve their performance dramatically when they are working with computers.

Papert asserts that schools must teach the *process* of learning. "When you learn to program a computer," he says, "you almost never get it right the first time. You must isolate and correct 'bugs.' The question to ask is: is it fixable? If this concept were generalized . . . we all might be less intimidated by our fears of 'being wrong.'"

In the course of their work with LEGO bricks and Logo, children find that they can complete projects that seemed, at first glance, to be impossibly complex. They learn to plan, to be patient, to brainstorm with their peers, and to look for new solutions when the old ones don't apply. They learn to tackle the problems of school, and of life, with creativity and confidence.

The Art of LEGO Bricks

Prominently displayed in the company's offices at Billund is a large LEGO brick creation that is part palace and part guitar, with a crashed helicopter and the Mona Lisa figuring mysteriously in the structure. Its name is *An Interhistorical Meeting Point*, and it is an architectural fantasy built by fourteen student architects from seven countries, in the course of a week at a workshop in Aarhus, Denmark in 1984.

The students chose the task of designing villas for four different personalities from vastly different ages and cultures: Leonardo da Vinci, M. C. Escher, Michael Jackson, and Julius Caesar. Each of the occupants were to have an individual residence, but their quarters had to come together on a central plaza—the meeting point of the title. Michael Jackson dwelt in a tower shaped like a guitar. Escher wandered a maze of staircases. Caesar's home was distinguished by a long colonnade. And the facade of Da Vinci's villa was adorned with his most famous portrait. A helicopter he designed lies crumpled on the ground after an unsuccessful test flight.

The *Interhistorical Meeting Point* was not the first project on which architecture and LEGO bricks had crossed paths. For some time, British architectural groups had held annual competitions in which their members were offered a pile of bricks, given a theme—such as "a monument to the Unknown Architect"—and within a few hours had to produce a structure. But in the summer of 1985 a more serious architectural event took place at the Pompidou Center in Paris, the opening of a traveling exhibit of thirty LEGO brick dream houses, designed by young European architects from ten countries. The exhibit was titled *"L'Architecture est un jeu . . . magnifique"* (Architecture is a . . . magnificent game). The exhibition has traveled to Switzerland, Belgium, Germany, Denmark, Italy, and Spain.

109

One of the dream houses designed for the traveling exhibition that opened in 1985 at the Pompidou Center in Paris, this imposing "Casa Weinbrenner" is the work of the German architect Hans Robert Hiegel. He described it as "a house to gather friends, a house to retreat into." The entire ground floor is a vast banqueting hall; the owner resides on the two top floors.

The rules of this game were simple: the architects were to imagine a client and design a dream house that would suit that person's character. The architects were allowed to give their fantasies free rein, the only restriction being that the designs had to be constructed (by the LEGO company's own model-building shop from the architects' plans) entirely out of regular LEGO bricks.

The exhibit was the surprise hit of the Paris summer, in fact, one of the most popular exhibitions in the eight-year history of the Pompidou Center, and has been drawing crowds wherever it is shown. Why an architectural exhibit made from toy bricks should become a huge popular success is a puzzle, but the reason people queued up to see it was that it revealed the secret life of architecture. Unlike the banalities of modern commercial architecture, as embodied in Manhattan today, here was a flowering of fantasies and dreams, and the public flocked to see what their world might look like if it could be remade in LEGO bricks.

The British architect Eric Owen Parry built
"Villa of the Physicists," which he imagined as an appropriate setting for Friedrich
Durrenmatt's play *The Physicists*. Parry has
said that building with LEGO bricks is similar to playing chess or composing music.

Designed by two architects from Frankfurt am Main, Jochem Jourdan and Bernhard Müller, "In the Real Nowhereland" condenses an entire fantasy town into a small space, through which a path meanders over steps, galleries, and bridges. The town is occupied by a family whose grandmother, a teller of fairy tales, lives in a blue tower. The architects call it "the scenery of the Grimm brothers."

The title of the exhibition was drawn from a 1923 essay by the French-Swiss architect Le Corbusier, in which he wrote, "Architecture is the skillful, exact and magnificent game of assembling volumes in light." The organizers of the show, Albert Roskam and Reyn van der Lugt of the Art Projects Foundation and Rotterdam Art Foundation, wrote: "The choice of LEGO bricks for building the thirty scale models of the villas fits in with Le Corbusier's vision of architecture. . . . We wanted to demonstrate both the serious and the play element of architecture."

The architects were delighted to take on the project. As a group of Dutch participants wrote: "The job of designing a LEGO brick villa will appeal to many an architect's imagination. Does it not offer a fantastic opportunity to build the house of one's dreams, expense no object, no bothersome rules and regulations, no annoying clients?" Working with LEGO bricks conferred the artistic freedom of play, the freedom to create the most impractical buildings. The architects were free to roam in the LEGO brick realm of pure inventiveness. For some, the project permitted a return to the reveries of childhood. "In planning my LEGO house," one

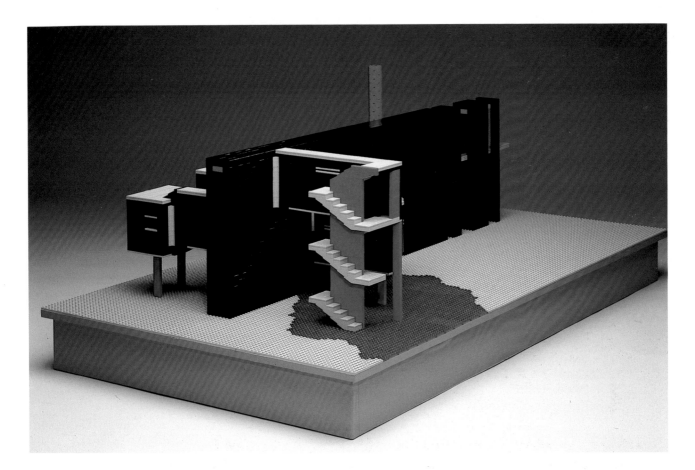

wrote, "I wanted to identify with the sandcastle builder of my childhood." And because the bricks are toys, they were the perfect material for architectural fantasies, puzzles, and puns. The unreal could take shape, the unbuildable could be built. One builder said that his plan was "to alternate the enigmatic with the credible."

The game of assembling dreams in LEGO bricks not only piqued the imaginations of the architects, it offered unique design possibilities. LEGO bricks are a superb material for serious building, and although they have definite limitations that force a builder to think in a special way, they also have certain virtues. The bricks are tiny bits of shape and color to be assembled piece by piece, which makes it a relatively simple task to create elaborate patterns of color and shapes. One of the architects wrote that the LEGO brick form of construction is ideal for exploring themes of rhythm and harmony, and he compared LEGO brick designs to the intricacies of music and chess.

Katia Lafitte, the French architect of "La Maison du Philosophe Dematerialisé," describes her creation as "black-sheathed, aloof, polished, poised, without balance, without rigidity, ordered without regulations." Entering the house necessitates a scary climb up an outdoor stairway without banisters.

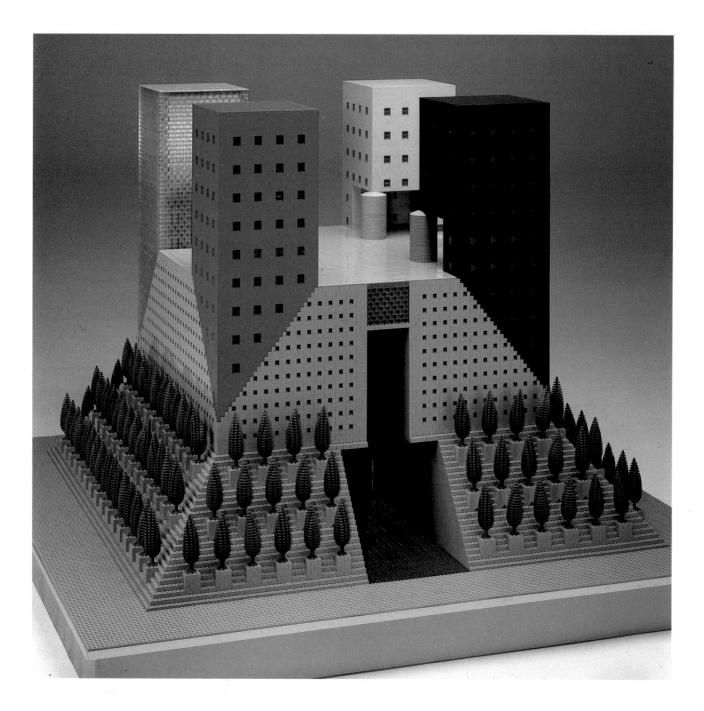

The architects responded to the project in many different ways. They dreamed their houses in a profusion of styles—Classical, Minimalist, Gothic, Palladian, Post–Modernist, and purely whimsical—while the imaginary clients included an existentialist, a pianist, a dematerialist philosopher, a reclusive billionaire, characters from fairy tales and modern fiction, and a lunatic. Some builders were most concerned with problems of architectural form, while others designed houses that were meditations on myth, the sea, childhood, or the passage of time.

Two decades before the Pompidou Center exhibit, the writer Norman Mailer used the medium of LEGO bricks to make a forceful statement about modern architecture. In 1965 Mailer constructed his vision of a vertical city of the future, a multicolored, twenty-thousand-brick model that stands over seven feet tall and about seven feet wide. A year later, a photograph of the model appeared on the dust jacket of Mailer's collection of essays, *Cannibals and Christians*. If ever a real city were built from the model, it would be about half a mile high, and would provide fifteen thousand homes, accommodating fifty thousand people. Mailer's thought was that the city might be built on Governor's Island in New York Harbor, a site currently occupied by the Coast Guard.

The Museum of Modern Art wanted to display Mailer's LEGO brick model, but it was impossible to move it out of his Brooklyn Heights apartment. It still occupies an honored spot at his picture window, overlooking Governor's Island, the harbor, and the sleek, blank towers that loom over lower Manhattan.

Although hundreds of architects have built with LEGO bricks, the bricks have not been widely used by artists. The paucity of colors and the strict standardization of shapes are apparently more burdensome limitations for artists than for architects. Finally, the bricks are of plastic, an inartistic material in the view of many—a view expressed by the French writer Roland Barthes in an essay on plastic: "In the hierarchy of the major poetic substances, it figures as a disgraced material." Nonetheless, the LEGO brick has been used by a few artists intrigued by the possibilities of artistic play.

"Villa of Insanity" is a complex construction designed by a Belgian, Jo Crepain. The four towers sit atop four great halls, illuminated by 444 windows in the gray walls. Each tower represents a state of insanity, and within each is played "its own music, endlessly repeated, filling the space."

Heinz Kleine-Klopries uses DUPLO bricks to create life-size sculptures that seem playfully friendly yet menacing at the same time. *Ikarus II* falls from the sky at left. Above is his work *Sculptor* and, opposite page, *Mounted Sculptor.*

One of these is the German artist Heinz Kleine-Klopries, who has built a series of large-scale DUPLO brick sculptures. His five-foot-tall *Sculptor* is a massive, square-headed DUPLO brick man holding in his arms a human figure made of clay. In another work, *Mounted Sculptor*, the DUPLO figure confronts a clay human seated on a pedestal. In both of the works the sculptor is the DUPLO man, whose shape is dehumanized and almost robot-like, yet childishly colorful, and almost gentle in its posture. Kleine-Klopries has also made a sculpture based on the Icarus myth, showing monumental DUPLO men—one of them is over ten feet tall—tumbling headlong to the earth like the ancient Greek boy who flew too close to the sun and melted his waxy wings.

116

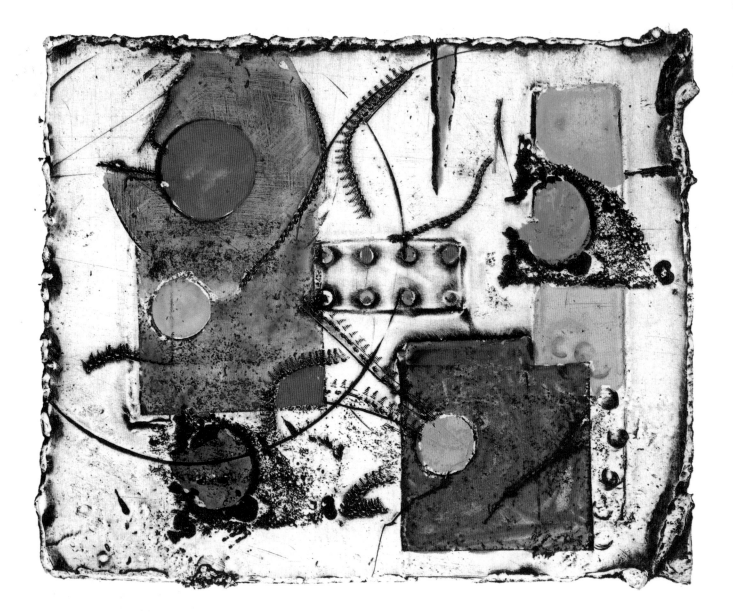

The Danish sculptor Robert Jacobsen made
an etching titled *Recycled LEGO* by first
pressing bricks and parts of molds onto a
copper sheet. He added lines with an
etching needle, pressed the copper onto
paper, and colored the paper by hand.

The Dutch architect Reinbern A. Jansma was delighted to rediscover his first architectural design—a two-brick villa he built with a LEGO set when he was four. His father had saved it for more than twenty years and, said the architect, "I was happy to be recognized so soon.... With LEGO I build my ego." Jansma feels that the villa's style "fitted my Calvinistic, modernistic Dutch background." He keeps another brick construction, a colorful cube, among mementos of his childhood (top).

119

Ancient Greek builders used decorative elements that look remarkably like the top surface of LEGO bricks. Lying on the ground amid the ruins of a temple, this stone block with 18 studs, called guttae, was originally fixed on the underside of the roof of the temple's portico. A person entering the temple would have seen it on looking up. The Greeks may not have built their temples with prototypes of the LEGO brick, but they did regard a block with neat rows of studs as an object of beauty.

The contemporary sculptures of Wolfgang Hahn, such as a stool partly enclosed in bricks, are not intended to be merely decorative. Instead, they startle the viewer by altering familiar objects in strange ways.

The artist who has made the most extensive use of LEGO bricks is the German sculptor Wolfgang Hahn, who has chosen to work with the bricks instead of more traditional materials. He takes his LEGO work quite seriously, which is to say that he regards it as close to playing, and he has written several short essays explaining his choice of material and his aesthetic of the LEGO brick. He admits that his medium is unusual, and one that may not offer all the artistic and physical satisfactions of sculpting in stone. In one essay he wrote, "At some time in his life, every sculptor dreams—like Michelangelo—of standing face to face with a massive block of marble and getting to work on it with hammer and chisel: a muscular giant in the grip of inspiration, forcing his will on the brittle material."

But the classic materials of sculpture inevitably produce a monumental style of art with an air of permanence about it, which Hahn believes does not reflect the true state of contemporary culture. The culture of the late twentieth century is provisional and ever-changing, as society itself undergoes rapid changes and seeks to understand them. "I don't think the present is the time for monumental art," he once wrote, "we are much too busy seeking a new understanding of ourselves to be able to afford that kind of thing. . . . So what we need to do is produce art on credit. But for that we need a 'recyclable material.'"

The search for a material that would reflect contemporary culture led Hahn to LEGO bricks. "I played with LEGO bricks as a child; it is a material of my generation," he wrote. "LEGO bricks satisfy all the demands a sculptor can make on a material. They are a raw material typical for our age. Form and function are identical—and an immense amount of creativity has gone into their development. . . . They provoke a playful work form, and they can be reused." And in a large understatement, he noted that "LEGO bricks have not yet turned up in the history of art," thus leaving him with complete freedom to do what he wished with them, without having the spirits of the old masters peering over his shoulder.

Wolfgang Hahn has built LEGO brick sculptures to fit the contours of spaces in various art galleries and other, less grand, exhibition spaces. He designed one sculpture for the corner in a university shower room—a space he liked because he was fascinated by the coldness of the tiles.

Hahn is perhaps the ideal artist to work in LEGO bricks because he approaches his work with total seriousness and total playfulness. He is an intriguing theorist who is also a jokester. Hahn's first idea for a LEGO construction was to build a cube, about six feet in each dimension, out of black, eight-stud LEGO bricks. It would have been the most massive LEGO brick construction ever built, and Hahn planned the project specifically to win the cube an entry in *The Guinness Book of World Records*—a dubious honor for a work of art, but that was exactly Hahn's intention, to question the nature of artistic achievement. He would also have succeeded in mocking Minimalism by creating a Minimalist work out of a toy; and by using LEGO bricks, he would erase the personality and authority of the artist. As one of his friends, an art critic, commented, "No future art historian would have been able to decide whether an identical cube were an authentic Hahn or an equally authentic duplicate." Hahn approached the LEGO company for the needed bricks, and at first they were receptive to the idea (which appealed to the company's

The stepped construction of transparent bricks glowing with the light of a television set inside it is part of a series of sculptures by Wolfgang Hahn called "Illuminations."

Very subtle color effects can be achieved with LEGO bricks, as in this realistic marlin, displayed like a fishing trophy at the company's headquarters in Billund.

own well developed sense of humor). But when they calculated that the project would require 1,600,000 bricks, weighing almost four tons, they had to refuse. So the LEGO cube never got off the drawing board.

In 1985 Hahn exhibited several LEGO brick sculptures, under the title "Illuminations," at the Massachusetts College of Art in Boston. The sculptures were hollow geometric forms, made from transparent bricks, with television sets inside illuminating them. One was a monolith that resembled a skyscraper, another was a rectangle that lay on its side on the floor, and the third was a monolith with an arm that enters the wall, suggesting the schematic shape of a stove and stovepipe.

The sculptures were displayed in a small, dark room with a curtained door. The only light came from the sculptures themselves. The impression was of entering the inner sanctuary of a temple to art, but the idols of this cult were made of LEGO bricks. And instead of flickering braziers there were flickering TV sets, emitting their eerie hum. The light was eerie as well, with its neutral silver muted and diffused by the transparent bricks. This strangely unsettling light in the temple of art was an effect that Hahn had planned. He said, "I had wanted to work with light for a long time, and the 'sterility' of the transparent bricks really inspired me."

Robert Jacobsen's twelve-foot-high tribute to the brick, entitled *LEGO*, was completed in 1976 and installed on the grounds of the Billund offices. The iron sculpture weighs three and a half tons.

LEGOLAND Park

The LEGO brick fulfills its ultimate destiny at LEGOLAND Park. A miniature version of the world (or some picturesque parts of it, at least) has been created entirely out of ordinary LEGO bricks, thirty million of them, at this twenty-five acre park just down the road from the company's headquarters in Billund. There the visitor can gaze on a forty-six-foot-high version of Mount Rushmore, set dramatically in the side of a cliff; an enormous statue of Sitting Bull; a Thai temple, one of the most beautiful buildings in the park, with its intricate pattern of colors; and the complex gantry of the launching pad at Cape Kennedy, with a space shuttle ready for flight. There are recreations of actual villages from Denmark, Finland, Sweden, and Norway; a replica of a charming section of Amsterdam overlooking a canal; and a view of the Rhine River with a mountain railway and a sidewheel riverboat, all constructed with meticulous accuracy on a scale twenty times smaller than life-size by the LEGO company's designers and master builders.

The scenes bustle with automated activity: Dutch windmills turn, bridges rise to allow boats to pass, a millrace turns a miniature waterwheel, trains shuttle back and forth. The Swedish village has a system of three locks that actually work, permitting miniature boats to descend in stages from the crest of a hill to the village harbor. Diminutive Welshmen browse at open-air bookstalls, two Dutch workmen haul a little stack of Gouda cheeses, a Norwegian mother wheels a baby in a tiny carriage, and red-coated horsemen gallop through the grounds of the Eremitage, the hunting lodge of the Danish royal family.

The four famous faces carved on South Dakota's Mount Rushmore—Washington, Jefferson, Theodore Roosevelt, and Lincoln—have been recreated at LEGOLAND by sculptor Bjørn Richter with 1.5 million standard LEGO bricks.

Amalienborg Palace, the royal family's Copenhagen residence, is the centerpiece of the park's model of part of the Danish capital.

There is a model of Copenhagen's Amalienborg Palace, accurate down to the decorative patterns in the pavement, and the LEGOLAND Park version of the Egyptian temple Abu Simbel reproduces not only the four gargantuan statues of Ramses II, but even the tiny hieroglyphics on the temple wall. Viewed from a few yards away, the models look amazingly real; on closer inspection the precise detail of the illusion becomes apparent, all, all made of tiny bricks—doorknobs, flower boxes, streetlamps, miniature window displays in the shops, and on the boats, little round life preservers, windlasses, and buoys (made from the heads of LEGO people). The realism extends even to the plant life in the park. In order to have trees and shrubs that are in perfect scale with the buildings, the park's gardeners have bred dwarf varieties that stand only a few feet tall but look fully grown. The total effect is startling—it is as if whole towns and their landscapes had been put under a spell that caused them to shrink.

129

Romance flourishes in the miniature villages of LEGOLAND Park. A bride and groom stand in front of a country church as a carriage lumbers up to take them to their wedding reception.

The park's designers go to great lengths to ensure the accuracy of their models. In order to make a scale model of this village mill, the designers took scores of photographs of the original mill and the surrounding area.

One of the most carefully constructed areas in the park is the model of parts of Copenhagen harbor, which was installed in 1984. Eight model builders labored for a year and a half to build it, using almost three million bricks. The harbor has 123 separate buildings, from the historic houses of the old Nyhavn district to the warehouses and oil tanks of the port's freight terminal. Among the forty-one ships the modelers built were a pair of three-masted sailing ships, the training ship *Danemark* and the royal yacht *Dannebrog*, with their full riggings. Two final touches were needed to complete the harbor scene: Amalienborg Palace, which had been installed eight years earlier, had to be turned around so that it would be correctly oriented to the harbor, and the famous statue of the Little Mermaid had to be installed on her rock in the harbor. At the opening ceremonies, the mayor of Copenhagen presented a miniature copy of the sculpture, made out of copper. This replica of the Mermaid is so small (it had to be on the same scale as the rest of the harbor) that it could not be made of LEGO bricks, and it enjoys the distinction of being the only object in LEGOLAND Park composed of a "foreign substance."

A large portion of LEGOLAND Park is devoted to a life-size recreation—not done in LEGO bricks—of a Wild West frontier town, dubbed LEGOREDO Town. The town has several shops, a jail, and a saloon with a buffalo head on the wall, globe lamps, and a coin-operated player piano with rolls that play ragtime numbers. A flesh-and-blood, gun-toting sheriff in a black leather vest presides over the town, occasionally "arresting" visitors and depositing them in the jail. Now and then gunfire erupts on the street as outlaws challenge the sheriff to a fight. Danish musicians in Western garb pluck out country tunes on banjos, fiddles, and guitars. Indian Chief "Playing Eagle" holds court next to a totem pole of LEGO bricks, his hair hidden beneath a feathered war bonnet. But his buckskin-clad Indian squaw is likely to be a fair, blonde Danish beauty. A printing press cranks out WANTED—DEAD OR ALIVE posters, and visitors can put on costumes and pose for photographs as a Civil War general or a country preacher. The Wild West is one of the most popular attractions of LEGOLAND Park.

The "Legold Mining Company" operates a train that runs through a stark landscape of mountains and brush, and into the tunnels and past the shafts of a gold mine. Another railroad, the Timber Ride, has cars that look as if they had been hewn from enormous logs. The line rolls past a cliff face where there is an enormous LEGO brick relief some one hundred and fifty feet long of Indians hunting buffalo.

The Timber Ride train speeds past the heroic LEGO brick relief of Indians hunting buffalo. Meanwhile, in nearby LEGOREDO Town, a costumed Dane acts out the role of Chief Playing Eagle in the park's affectionate recreation of the American Old West.

Bjørn Richter's massive sculpture of Sitting Bull was two years in the making. The sculptor posed with the completed work in his studio, after which it was reassembled section by section for installation in the park. The dedication ceremony for the statue was attended by a representative of the Sioux tribe.

The two largest constructions in the park, Mount Rushmore and a statue of Sitting Bull, took years to complete. Both were executed by the Danish sculptor Bjørn Richter, who was inspired to portray Sitting Bull after he visited the American West and became interested in the history and culture of the American Indians. It took Richter two years to design and build his tribute to Sitting Bull, which is over forty feet high and required one and a half million bricks. It was fitting that LEGOLAND Park made its own version of Mount Rushmore, since the original portrait busts in South Dakota were hewn out of the rock by the great Danish sculptor Gutzon Borglum.

Overleaf: A visit to LEGOLAND Park is akin to going around the world in a day. The tourist who cannot make it to Egypt to see the temple of Abu Simbel will find a perfectly acceptable LEGO brick copy at the park.

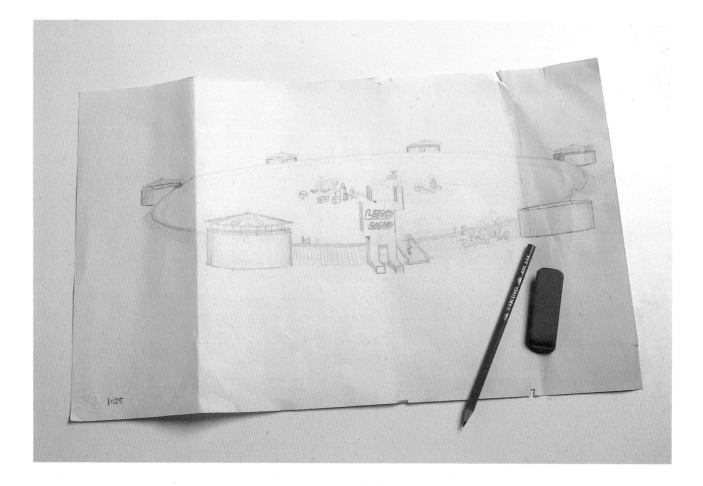

The original plan for the park, sketched in pencil by Arnold Boutrup in the mid-1960s, called for a simple layout with only a few models on display. The company was astounded by the instant success of the park, which has grown in popularity and in the number of attractions since 1968.

GKC got the idea for LEGOLAND Park when he noticed that visitors to the LEGO plant were always fascinated by the studio where promotional models for window displays were made. His original plan for putting the models on display was modest. As GKC recalled, "What I had in mind at first was something in the way of a large open-air show, maybe the size of a football field, where a pensioner couple could sell tickets and perhaps run a small cafeteria. But when we eventually, in the mid-1960s, got down to putting our ideas on paper the plan and our ambitions had grown. But just about everybody shook their heads—it was a Utopian notion to think you could set up a tourist attraction in the middle of the bleak Jutland moors, where people had no desire to come. But I've inherited a good chunk of my father's obstinacy."

He asked a Copenhagen window designer, Arnold Boutrup, to submit designs for an entire theme park of LEGO models. Boutrup laid out a set of miniature LEGO brick towns on a three-acre site, which opened in 1968. The park was an immediate and surprising success. "During the few months the season lasted," GKC said, "we had no fewer than 625,000 paying visitors. It knocked all our planning over the moon; at the most, we had expected only half that figure." In less than twenty years the size of LEGOLAND Park has increased more than eightfold, and, with about 900,000 visitors a year, it is Denmark's most popular tourist attraction outside of Copenhagen.

Boutrup says, "The park communicates the boundless possibilities provided by the brick . . . the challenge it presents to the imagination." And he took the word "challenge" seriously. Instead of constructing imaginary buildings and towns, Boutrup decided that it would be more interesting and appealing to recreate actual places. He wanted to demonstrate that there is virtually nothing in the world that cannot be reproduced in LEGO bricks, if only you try hard enough (and have a LEGO factory at your disposal). The rules of this project are strict: from the start the builders have been forbidden to use any custom-made

elements (with the exception of specially colored bricks) or any structural supports. They must use only the components that a child would get in the standard box of bricks. The builders are allowed to glue the bricks together, but only to assure that the constructions hold together through handling, transport, and the harsh Danish winters.

One of the most influential creators of LEGOLAND Park was Dagny Holm, a chief designer at the model shops in Billund until her retirement in 1986. Before she was invited to join the design team that made the company's exhibition and window displays, in the early 1960s, Holm had sculpted in clay, and she was not very enthusiastic about working in the more limited medium of plastic bricks. But after working with the bricks for a while she found that they offered artistic possibilities of their own that called for a different way of thinking about forms. Creating was not a matter of molding, as it is in clay, but of making patterns, an artistic method she compared to working embroidery. It was also matter of thinking in rectangles, the basic LEGO brick shape. Everything she built had to be made up of a set of rectangles, so fashioning curves required tricking the eye of the beholder.

The two creative spirits behind the formation of the park were Dagny Holm, who supervised the LEGO brick construction of many of the buildings and other sculptures, and Arnold Boutrup, the original designer, both photographed in 1968, the year the park opened. Dagny Holm stands next to a replica of a Norwegian stave church. Remarkably, only standard LEGO elements are used in all models, including the large exhibition pieces created for LEGOLAND and the traveling World Shows.

When she grasped the style of this kind of sculpture it became something of an obsession. In a 1980 interview she said, "I saw everything in those bricks. Even on a tram in Copenhagen I would be looking at people and calculating how many bricks for that nose, how many for that face." Holm's first LEGO brick model shook up the design team, which at that time was a rather staid group: she made a chicken on wheels. But her approach to the medium, a combination of realism and a droll sense of humor, set the style for the company's modelers.

Dagny Holm's great achievement is LEGOLAND Park. More than half of the park's models were built by her or under her direct supervision. It was a monumental task, not just in terms of dogged hard work, but in the unflagging ingenuity Holm showed in maintaining the freshness and charm of the displays.

Constructing a village from LEGO bricks is no simple feat for the design staff. In order to recreate the Swedish village, for example, designers visited the actual town, where they took thousands of photographs from every angle, and carefully measured everything in sight—houses, roads, bridges, church towers, and all the features of the natural landscape. Back at the studio they constructed a scale model of the village and its setting out of plaster, clay, and wood. Each building was then sketched out on special graph paper and assigned to a builder.

In the Miniland section of the park, villages have been meticulously constructed. The Rhine village includes a ferry wending its way along the river.

The model builders can recreate buildings of any architectural style and period with striking accuracy, from an elegant royal Danish hunting lodge to a rustic Welsh village.

Realism was not the only goal of Holm and the other master builders, for the park is more than a mere recreation of the world, it is a special view of the world. At LEGOLAND Park, life is a comical pageant that gently mocks the notion of ambition and go-getting. The railroads run in circles and the tugboats tug their weightless loads, to no purpose beyond entertainment. The work of the world becomes a carnival of quaint motions. The little people of LEGOLAND Park fish, hunt, and stroll the beautiful streets. Some people work, but a lot of the labor takes place on boats where the men just ride around all day. And if you could get a very close look at the populace, you would see that they all wear permanent grins, with the possible exception of the Germans, who seem to go about their business seriously. Holm created an especially charming nighttime atmosphere. At night in LEGOLAND Park, a myriad of lights twinkle in the houses, where, no doubt, a thousand festivities are going on, as the people prepare for another day of fishing, hunting, and aimless strolling along their perfect boulevards.

145

Overleaf: A bird's-eye view of LEGOLAND Park from its highest ride shows the sprawling layout of small-scale attractions, with the long low roofs of the full-size LEGO plant in the background.

Animal figures, a specialty of the model builders, are a great hit with children. The life-size giraffe, a prominent figure in the LEGOLAND Safari landscape, can be clearly seen in the aerial photo at the upper right. Approaching the giraffe, an electric car from the park's Traffic School moves along a course that simulates realistic traffic situations. Children between the ages of eight and twelve who have obeyed the traffic rules can earn a "license" after twenty minutes of driving.

The model builders are also adept at creating animals. Children, of course, are fascinated by animals, so there is a constant demand for them for window displays as well as for LEGOLAND Park, and the vivid LEGO brick colors might have been invented for modeling animals. Giraffes, elephants, flamingos, ostriches, gorillas, crocodiles, and lions are just a few of the beasts the modelers have contributed to the LEGO menagerie. In animal sculptures, the sculptor Bjørn Richter has achieved amazingly subtle effects with the LEGO colors, such as a yellow-and-black bumble-bee with delicate, transparent wings.

148

Dagny Holm and her crack team of model builders display a small sampling of their creative master-pieces—castles, churches, a Moorish palace, and a host of animals.

The workshops in Billund and the United States create the models for the World Shows, the models of historic buildings, spaceships, vehicles, and great inventions that tour department stores and shopping malls promoting LEGO toys. The leaning tower of Pisa, the White House, the U.S. Capitol, a thirty-foot Statue of Liberty, a London double-decker bus, Lindbergh's *Spirit of St. Louis*, and life-size mock-ups of a space cap-sule's control center are just a few of the models that have struck awe in the hearts of shoppers— "They did *that* out of LEGO bricks!?". Some of the models, such as the Capitol and the White House, are so large that they have to be shipped in sections.

An astronaut, floating weightless in space, enthralls a visitor at a World Show. The company's model builders have recreated, in life size, the command module of a space vehicle, complete with blinking control panels.

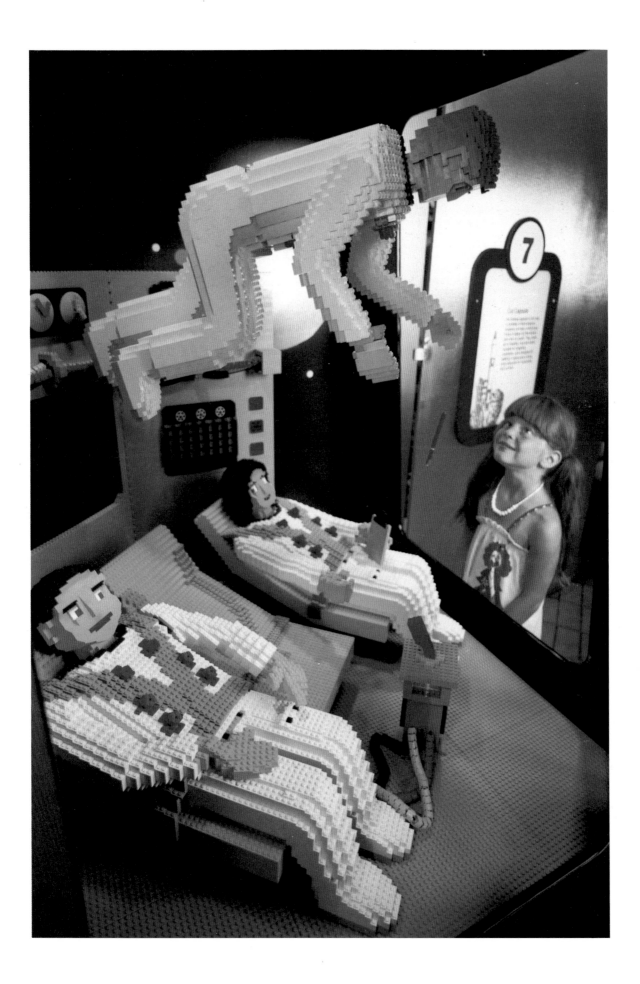

The model builders also constructed, from the architect's plans, the thirty "dream houses" for the architectural exhibit at the Pompidou Center—a feat they accomplished in a mere seven weeks. For the èntrance to the exhibit one of the modelers created three remarkably lifelike LEGO brick mosaic portraits of Le Corbusier, working from photographs.

Superb LEGO models have also been created by the British modelers, working at the company's offices in Wales. The British models have a theatrical air about them, undoubtedly because the chief British model maker also designed sets for a theater company. David Lyall, who retired in 1983 after more than two decades of working for LEGO, created some of the company's most memorable models. His own favorites were a copy of the Irish State Coach (which he was able to reproduce after only one day of studying and sketching the original) and a treatment of a traditional English theme, St. George slaying the dragon. Also in the line of traditional English topics, Lyall created a very merry Old King Cole

The LEGO company's British model builders fashioned Buckingham Palace for an advertisement and a picnic scene from *The Wind in the Willows* for pure whimsy.

sitting on his throne, and a LEGO brick tableau of King Arthur drawing the sword Excalibur from its stone. The tableau has an unmistakably theatrical quality: the wizard Merlin watches Arthur from a balcony above him, while seven other characters look on. To the rear a castle looms up on a hilltop, in perfect scale and perspective with the heroic scene in the foreground.

"It's a very exciting job," he once said in an interview, "I regard it more as an art medium than a children's play brick now." Before coming to the LEGO company he had worked in an advertising agency, so over the years he was given the job of making models for magazine ads. In 1982 he created a model of Buckingham Palace for an ad with the headline, supposed to be uttered by Prince Charles to his infant son: "Jolly good, William. Now make Daddy's motorcar." But his real talent was carica- ture, a talent he displayed in a 1981 ad with LEGO brick lampoons of three British political leaders under the headline "In the toy market, there's no question who's the leader." Lyall portrayed a bushy-maned Michael Foot, a jowly, beetle-browed Denis Healey, and a square-jawed Tony Benn, who smokes a pipe emitting a thin plume of smoke formed by a delicately balanced stack of transparent bricks.

Lyall's successor, John Duffield, is another adept caricaturist. In one of his ads he created a craggy-faced Arthur Scargill, the union leader, and three eccentric bobbies. He built a dinosaur for a LEGO World Show, that was twelve feet long and seven and a half feet high, with a moving head, flashing red eyes, and a jaw that opens and shuts as the beast roars. One of his finest creations was a series of LEGO brick illustrations of *Wind in the Willows*, depicting Mole's home and his picnic by the river. For Mole's house Duffield created a roaring yellow-and-red-brick fire and a beautifully patterned rug. The picnic menu included a bottle of pop, bread, cheese, and a tomato, served from a picnic basket on a checkered cloth. For his outing on the river, Mole brought along rod and reel, and rubber wading boots, all done in bricks, of course. Mole himself is an adorable character in a nifty blue jacket. Duffield's sequence tells the story charmingly.

The hallmark of Dagny Holm's models is the sense of humor they show in depicting daily life in LEGOLAND Park. In the hands of Duffield and Lyall, the LEGO brick acquired a distinctly British visual wit that nicely complements the Danish talent for creating a world that smiles at itself.

In the chronicle of twentieth-century inventiveness, the LEGO brick surely has a place on the roll of honor. Its design is ingenious—few objects are as elegantly simple yet as full of possibilities. Not as useful, perhaps, as the jet engine or the computer, the brick nonetheless ranks high on the scale of things that make life fun. It beguiles the imaginations of children and adults alike, who find that a pile of LEGO bricks is an irresistible invitation to create. At LEGOLAND Park there is an area set aside where visitors of any age can try their hand at building with LEGO bricks. Here at outdoor tables parents, grandparents, and children can be found collaborating on spur-of-the-moment constructions, with bricks provided by the park. Some attempt to copy, on an amateur's scale, the impressive structures of the master builders that they have just seen in the park, while others make cars, birds, skyscrapers, or perhaps the ferryboat that carried them to Jutland—with the bricks they can make almost anything. All lose themselves in the reverie of playful creativity that LEGO bricks induce, when, for a few moments, the world shrinks to the dimensions of a little brick house, and the colors of the world are vivid and full of youthful joy.

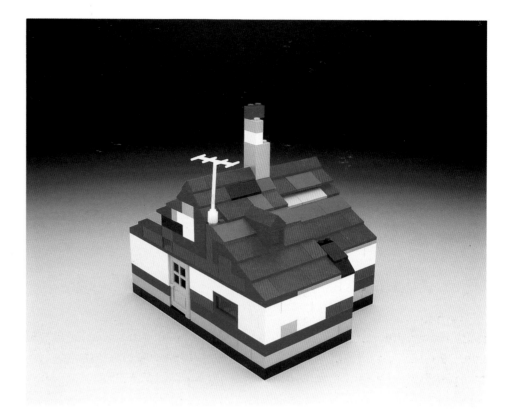

Building Instructions

The LEGO company has created thousands of models for children to build with their bricks and related elements. The instructions for assembling the models are among the finest in the toy industry, remarkably clear and easy to follow, no matter what the builder's language: the instructions use only pictures and no words. Since LEGO products are sold worldwide, the instructions can be immediately understood in any country. As examples of the graphic arts, the model plans have great visual charm and might even be called beautiful.

The instructions consist of a series of steps in which a model grows from a single element into a finished house, train, car, or functioning machine with motor, gears, and drive belt. By carefully examining the illustration for each step, the builder sees what pieces should be added at that step and precisely where to put them. Following the instructions requires concentration and attention to details, but LEGO builders don't find this a tedious chore—they become absorbed and excited as they see their models take shape step by step.

The instructions at right show how to build a scale that actually works. The little scissors symbol indicates that the curved section should be cut out of the sheet of paper and attached to the scale with the pegs. A child can then place an object on the platform at the top and weigh it. On the following pages are instructions for assembling a truck or van with louvered windows, an airplane, a forklift truck, a lunar exploration vehicle, a spaceship, and a cabin cruiser complete with pilot and passenger.

160

1

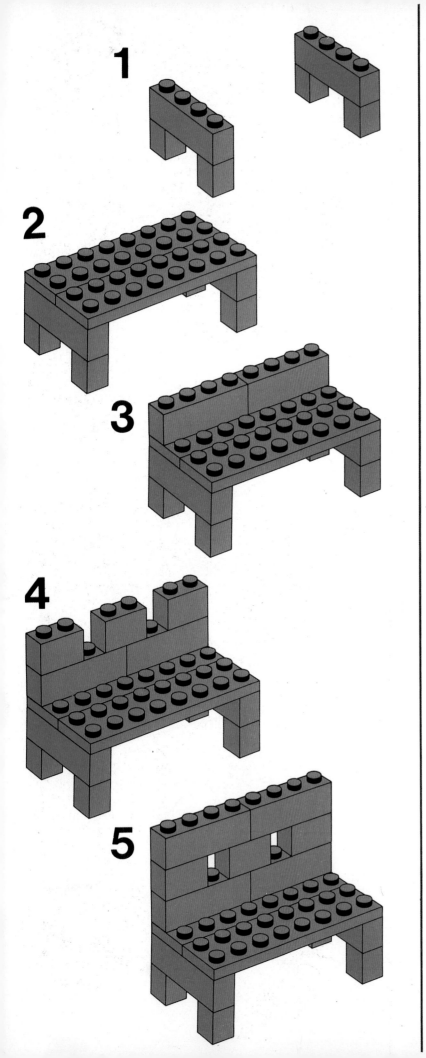

2

3

4

5

1

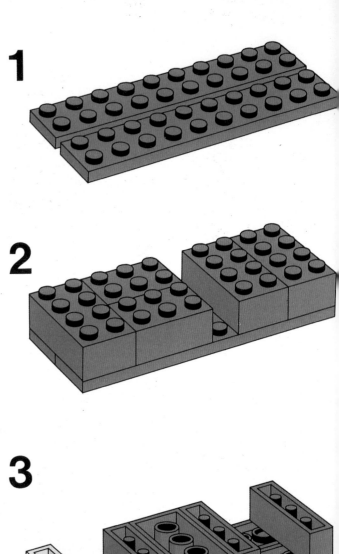

2

3

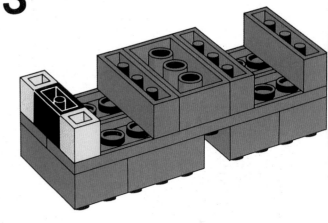

4

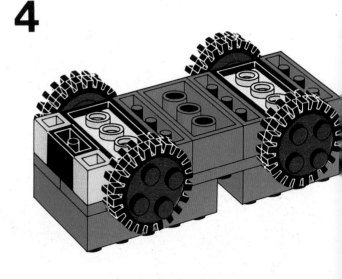

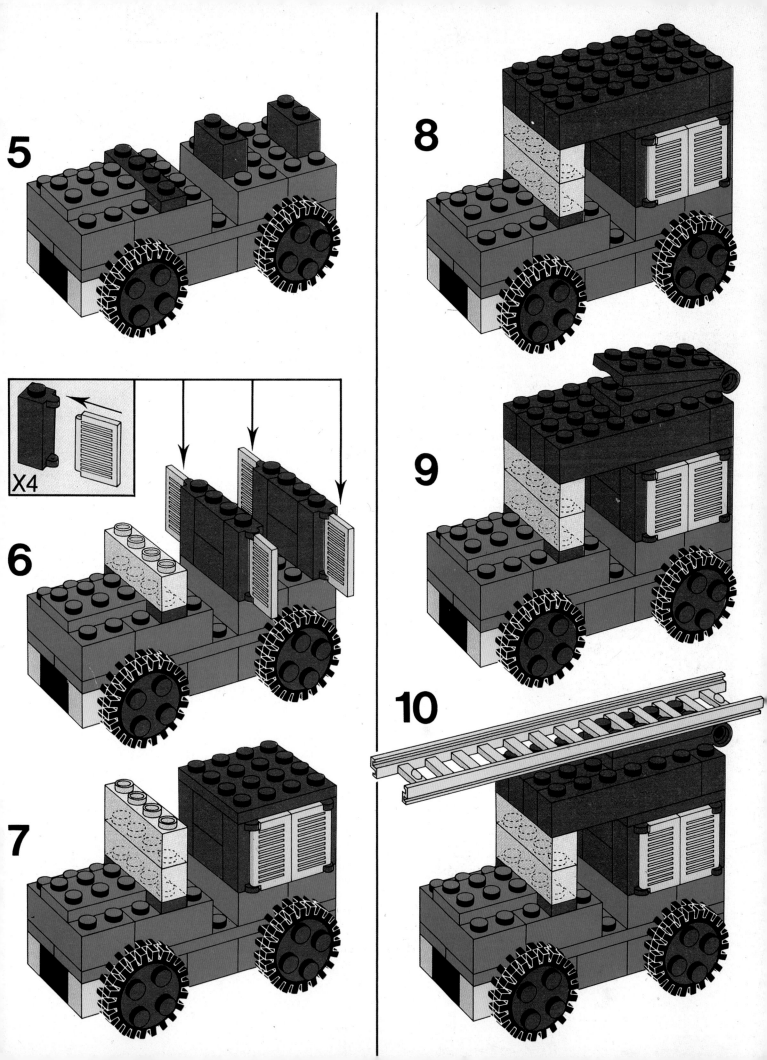

5

6

X4

7

8

9

10

1

2

3

4

5

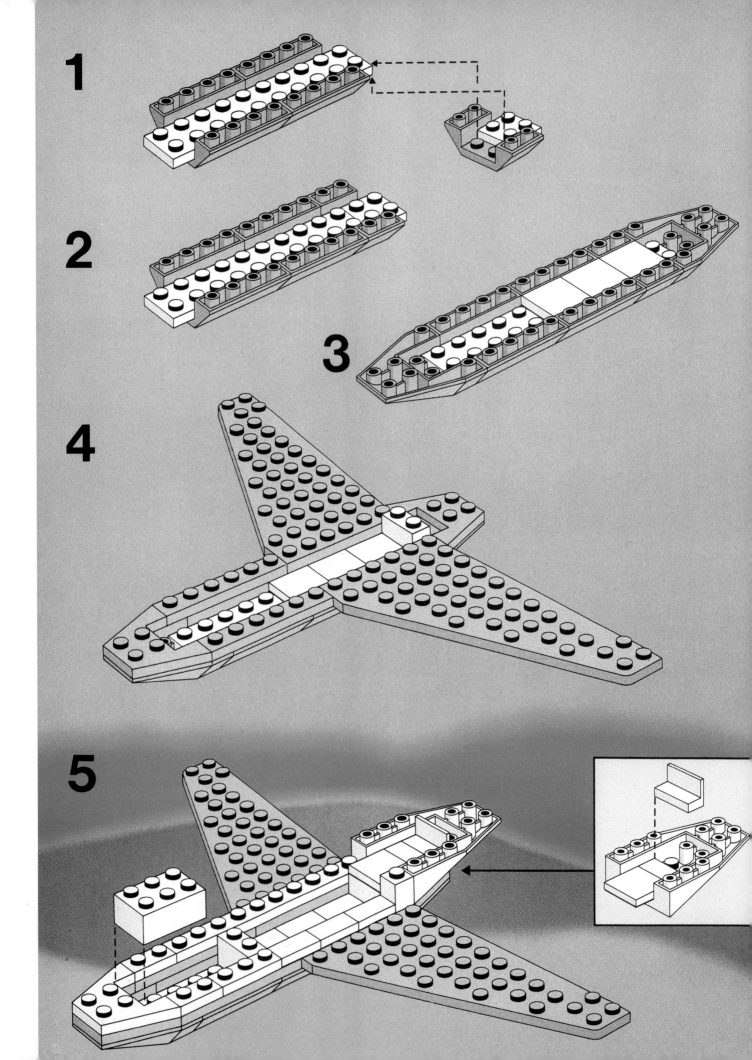

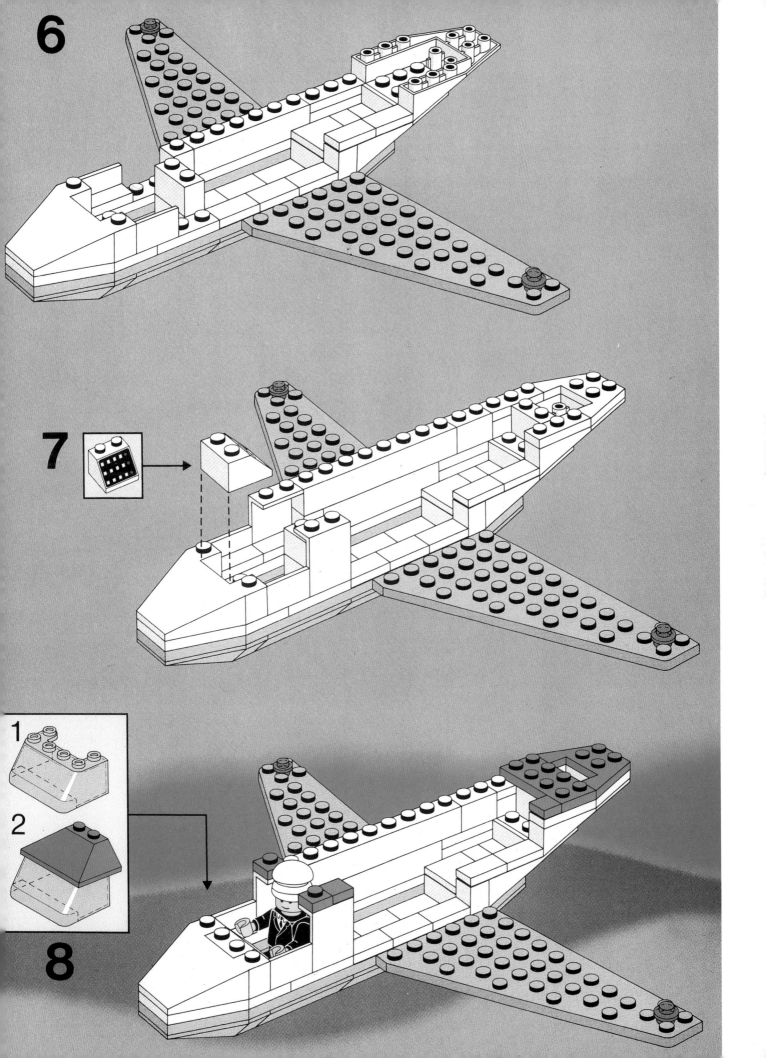

6

7

8

1

2

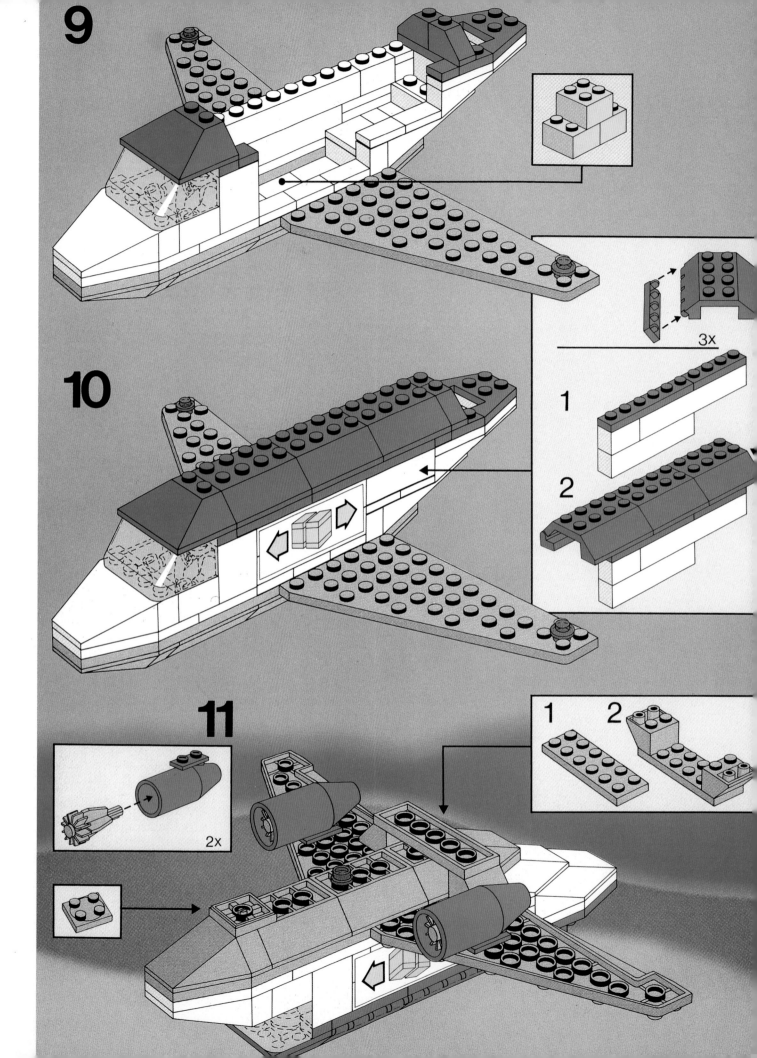

9

10

3x

1

2

11

1   2

2x

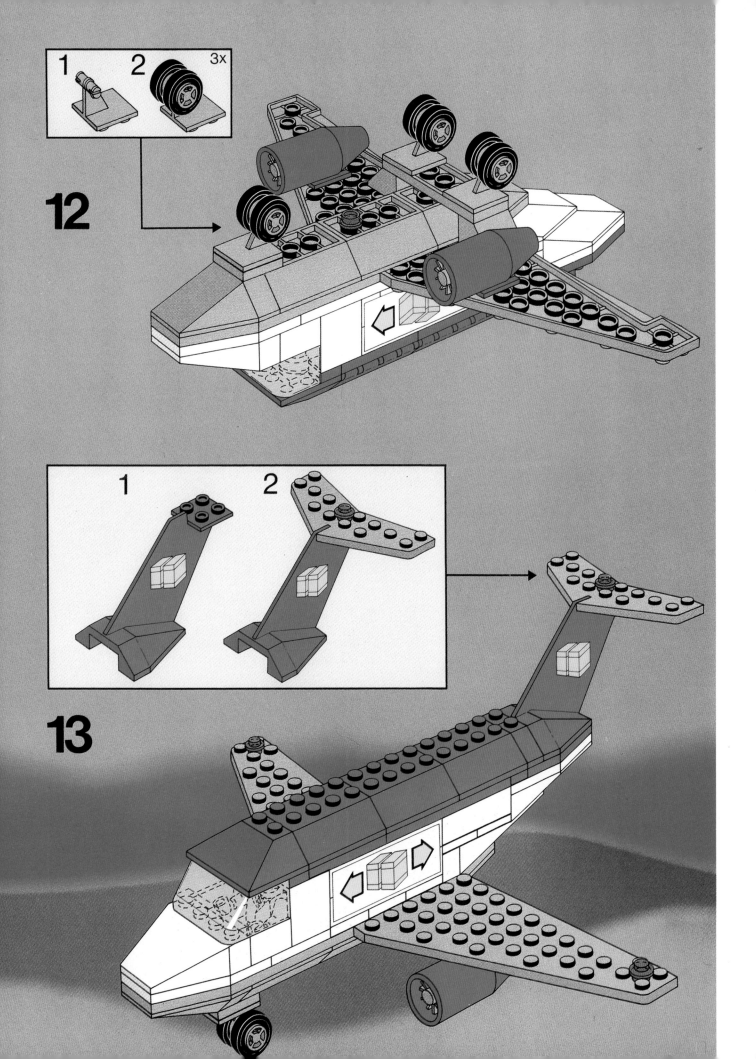

1 2 3x

12

1 2

13

1

2

3

4

5

6

7

8

1
2
3

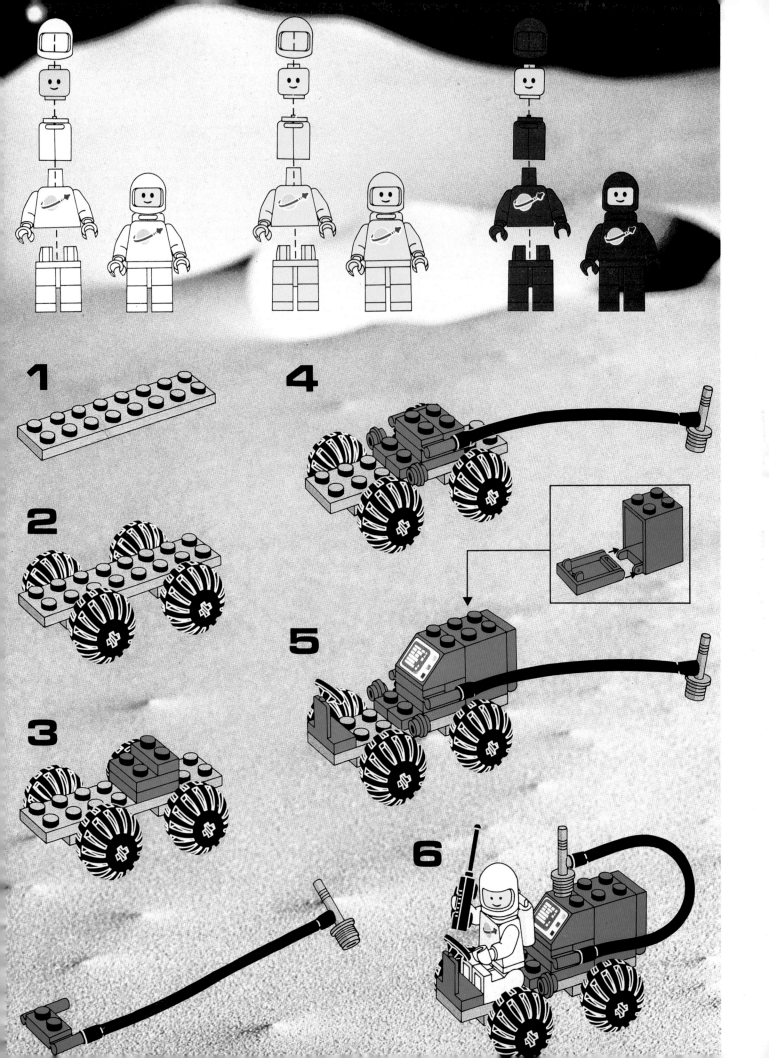

1

2

3

4

5

6

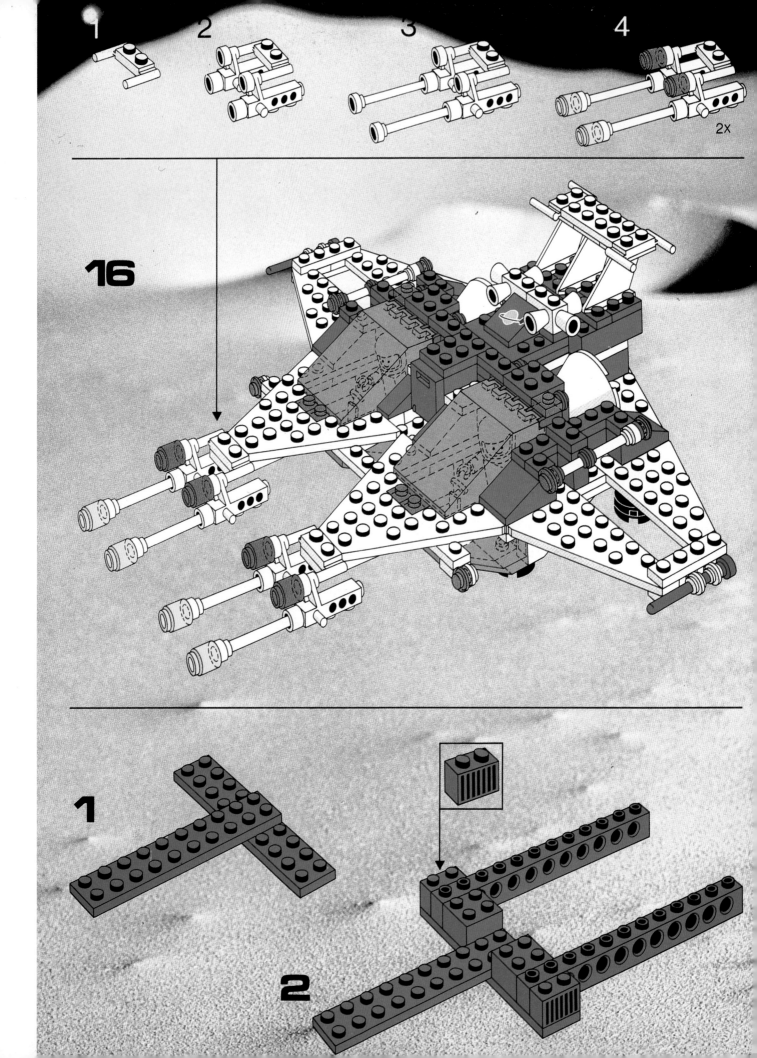

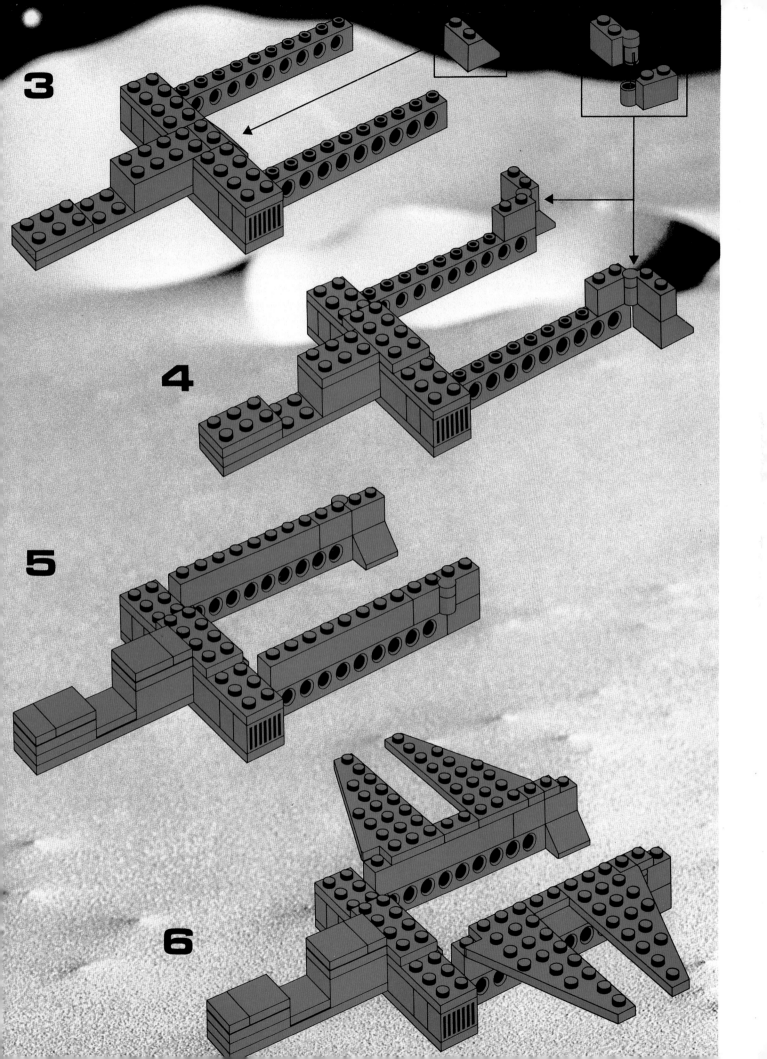

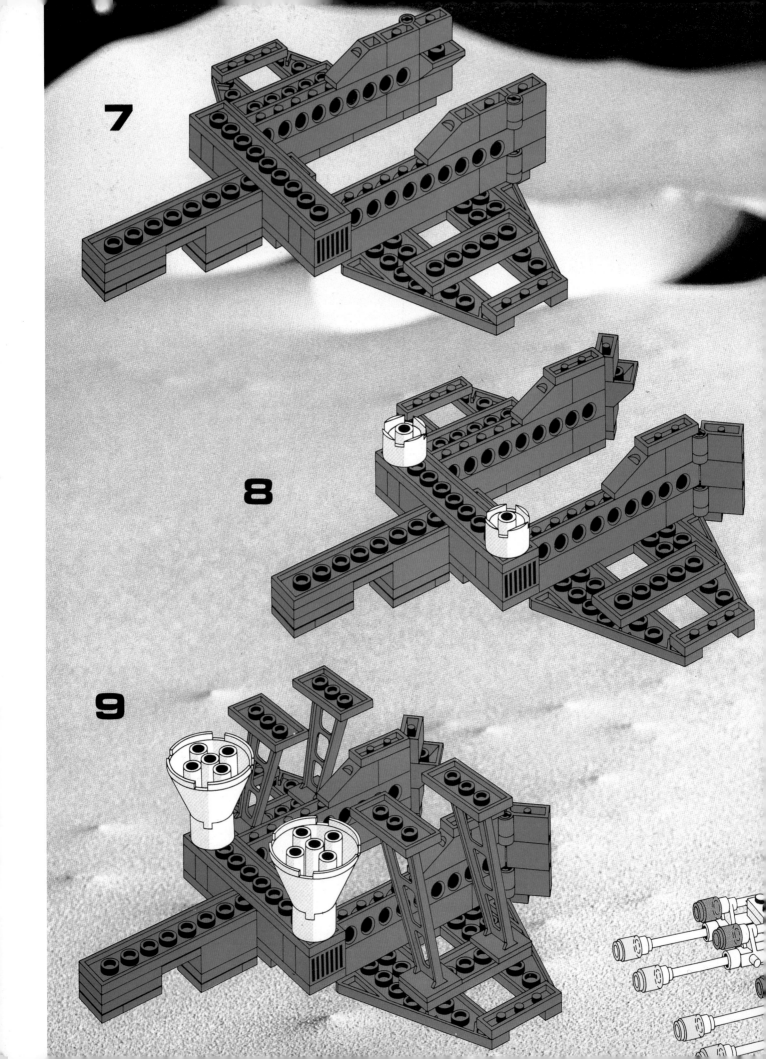

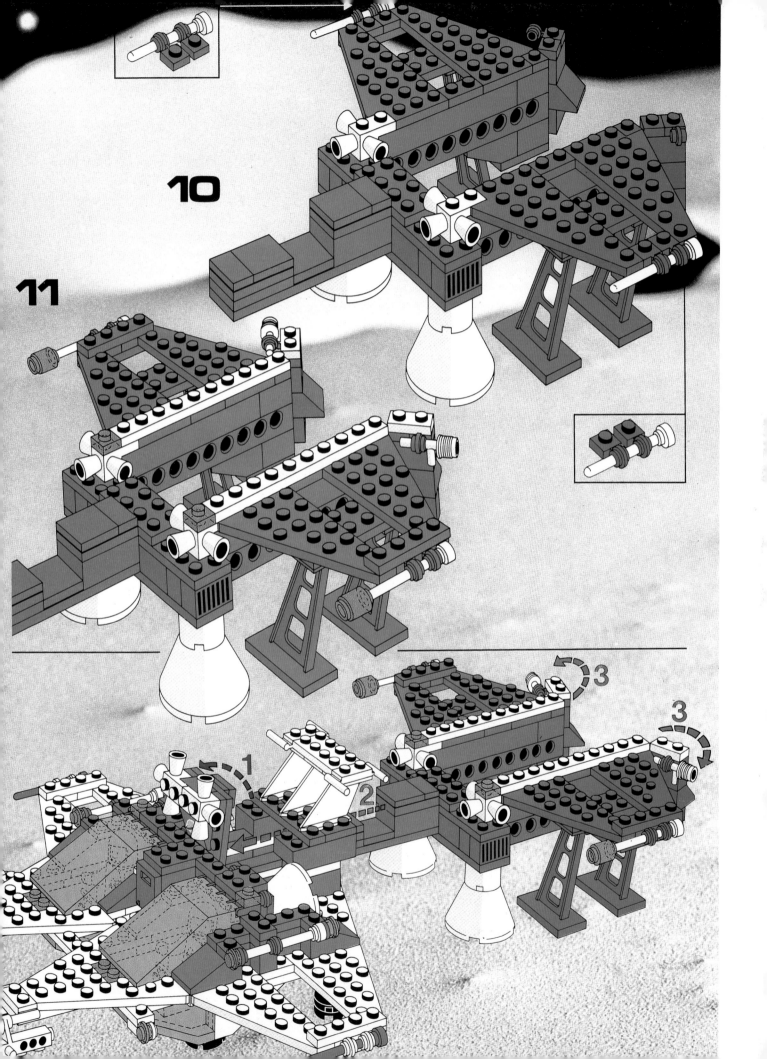

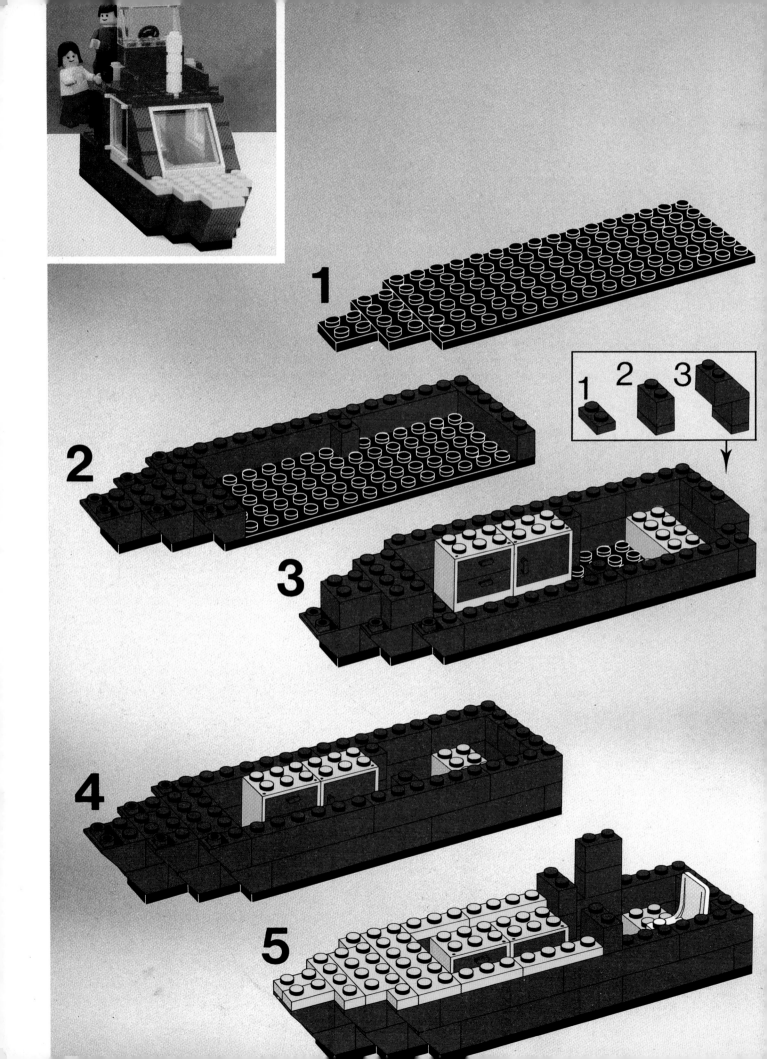

1

2

3

1 **2** **3**

4

5

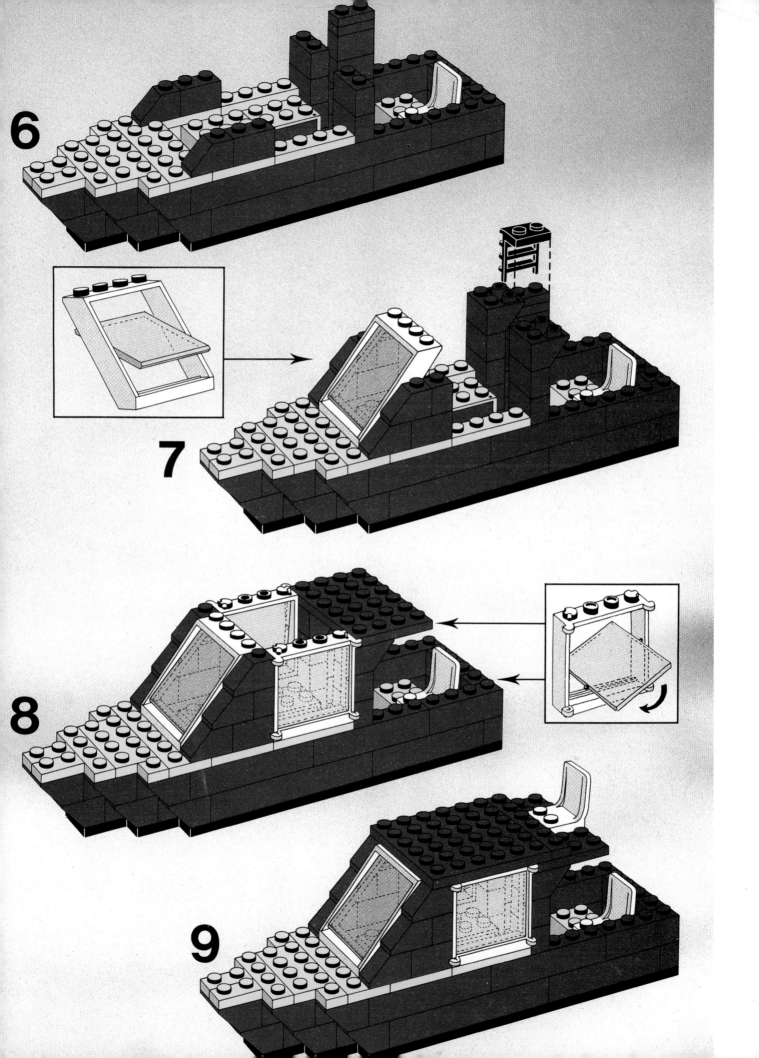

6

7

8

9

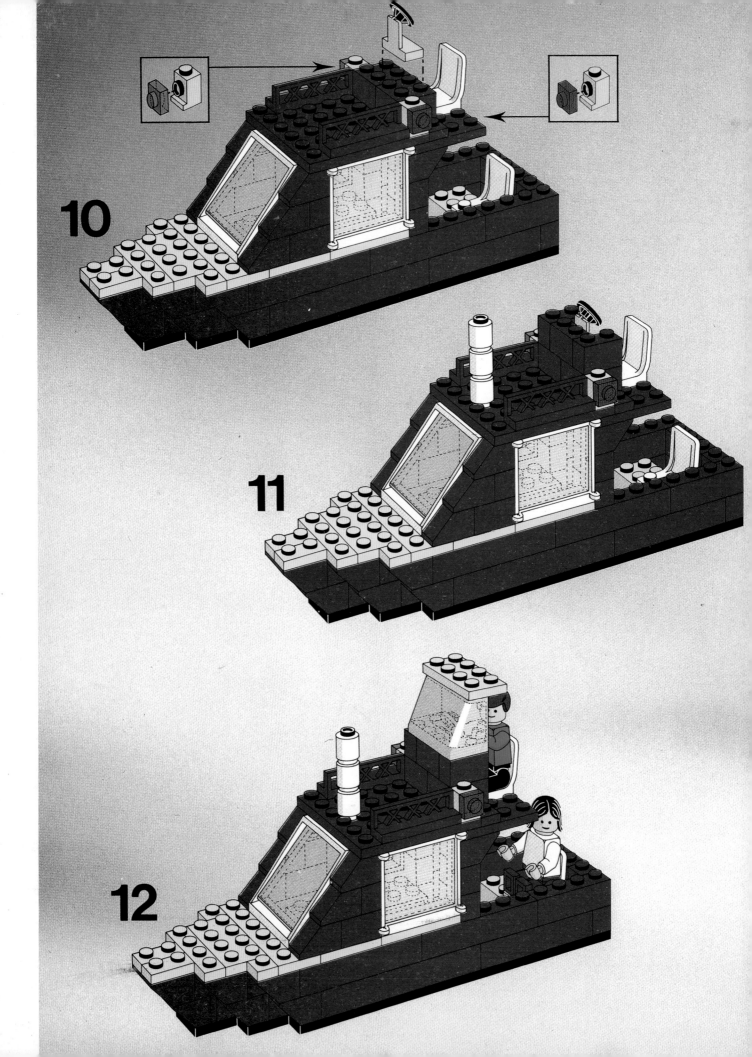

10

11

12